Recipes
& Recollections
of My Greek-American Family

ELAINE SCHMITZ

PHAROS PUBLISHING™

Recipes & Recollections of My Greek-American Family by Elaine Schmitz

Pharos Publishing
Post Office Box 1976
San Ramon, CA 94583-1395 U.S.A.

Paperback edition
ISBN: 978-0-615-31578-2

Cover and book design by DesignForBooks.com

Printed in China

Photo credits
Cover: Background, iStock©HowardOates; inset Steve Schmitz; olive branch: iStock©assalve. Page ii, iStock©hroe; pages iv–v, iStock©andriybozhok; page 15, iStock©Elenathewise; page 39, cloves, iStock©egal; page 123, iStock©timsa. Food photography throughout book by Steve Schmitz.

DEDICATION

To my husband, Steven, who encourages me to write;
To my children, Charles, Sally, Noah, and Darshan, who have always
loved my family's Greek cooking; and
To my grandchildren, Lila, Rubi, Asher, Maranatha, Isaac, Natasha,
Kai, and those yet born, for whom this book was written.

Contents

Acknowledgements   xiii

Introduction: A Taste for Nostalgia   1

    A FAMILY OF COOKS   2

I   **The Early Carlos Cooks**   5

    GLIEKO   5

      Eleni's Grapefruit Spoon Sweets—Glieko   7

    PETER CARLOS' SNACK SHACK BURGERS   8

      Peter Carlos' Snack Shack Hamburgers   10

    AND THEY HAULED PETER OFF TO JAIL   11

    CRETAN COOKING   16

      Eleni's Kallitsounakia   17

II   **The Early Manolakas Clan**   21

    LOUKOUMADES   21

      Despina's Loukoumades—Honey Balls   24

    PAXIMADIA   26

      Despina's Paximadia   27

    SAM MANOLAKAS' FLY TRAP   29

    VISITING MY OLD AUNTIE   30

      Stamatia's Koulourakia   32

THE YAYA WARS   33
   Despina's Keftaides—Greek Meat Balls   37
   Eleni's Baklava   38

III My Mother's Michigan Kitchen   41

MY MOTHER LEARNS TO COOK   41
   Angela's Chicken Pilafi   43
   Angela's Baked Chicken Oregani   44

A WORD ABOUT MY FATHER: WHAT'S IN A NAME?   45

SUMMERTIME BARBECUE   48
   Connie's Arni Souvlakia—Shish Kebab   50
   Connie's Greek Barbecued Chicken   51
   Connie's Broiled or Barbecued Fish   52

MORE SUMMER COOKING   53
   Angela's Pastitsio   54
   Angela's Stuffed Tomatoes and Green Peppers   56
   Eleni's Tiropites—Greek Cheese Puffs   59
   Angela's Peach Cobbler   61
   Angela's Fassolakia—Braised Green Beans   62

THE STRAW, THE BEAN, AND THE COAL   63
   Angela's Fassolourizo—Black Eyed Beans and Rice 66
   Angela's Fahki—Lenten Lentil Soup   67

KITCHEN CAPERS   67
   Angela's Spanakorizo—Spinach and Rice   69

IV Home for the Holidays   73

THANKSGIVING   73
   Angela's Candied Yams   74
   Angela's Cranberry Sauce   75
   Eleni's Turkey Gravy   76

Eleni's Greek Stuffing   78

CHRISTMAS   79
Eleni's Kourembiethes—Butter Tea Cookies   80
Angela's Kourembiethes—Butter Tea Cookies   81

NEW YEAR'S AND ST. BASIL'S DAY   82
Eleni's Vasilopita and Pascha Kouloures
—New Year's and Easter Bread   83

EASTER   85
Eleni's Yaourti—Greek-Style Yogurt   86

A DETROIT EASTER REVISITED   88
Kathryn's Taramasalata—Fish Roe Dip   89
Kathryn's Spanakopita—Spinach Pie   91
Kathryn's Galatoboureko   93
Kathryn's Koulourakia   95

V **My Mother's California Kitchen**   97

EVERYDAY FARE   97
Eleni's Youvarlakia
—Meatballs with Egg/Lemon Sauce   99
Angela's Greek Side Dish Pasta   100
Angela's Eggs with Zucchini   101

MY DAD THE SAILOR   102
Psari Plaki—Baked Fish with Vegetables   104

ANGELA'S ENTERTAINING   105
Angela's Taramasalata—Fish Roe Dip   106
Angela's Zucchini Casserole   107
Angela's Tourlou—Roasted Vegetables   108
Angela's Spanakopita—Spinach Pie   109
Angela's Moussaka—Eggplant Casserole   111

SUNDAY LUNCH   112
   Summer Sunday Lunch   114

A FIG JAM   115
   Angela's Fig Jam   117

LOST RECIPES   118
   Tootsie's Kolokithopita—Pumpkin or Squash Pita   119
   Tootsie's Bamias—Braised Okra   121
   Chubby's Karidopita—Walnut Cake   122
   Minnie's Skordalia
   —Garlic Sauce with Blanched Almonds   123
   Despina's Theples—Honey Curls   124
   Minnie's Copenheim   125

GREEK SALAD   126
   Angela's Greek Salad   127

FOUR BEAN SALAD   128
   Angela's Four Bean Salad   129

RICE PUDDING   128
   Angela's Rice Pudding   130

ROAST LEG OF LAMB   131
   Angela's Roast Leg of Lamb—Arni Psito 132
   Angela's Lamb and Orzo Roasted in the Pan 133

MY BROTHER AND SISTER-IN-LAW   133
   Poula's Ravani   135
   Maritza's Karidopita—Nut Cake   137

VI My Greek Kitchen   139
   Eleni's Koulourakia   140

RECIPE CREEP   142
   Eleni's Galatoboureko   143

Angela's Galatoboureko   144

YANKEE POT ROAST   145
Angela's Yankee Pot Roast   146

FORAGING FOR FOOD   146
Despina's Dolmadakia me Avgolemono
—Stuffed Grape Leaves with Egg/Lemon Sauce   147
Elaine's Dandelion Greens   149

COMMUNAL COOKING: A WORD OF ADVICE   151
Angela's Sesame Koulourakia   152
Angela's Fenikia with Nuts   153

GREEK INSPIRATION   154
Elaine's Lemon Roasted Potatoes   155
Elaine's Beet Salad   156
Elaine's Feta Omelet   157
Elaine's Dolmata Salata   158
Elaine's Broiled Calf's Liver   159

AVGOLEMONO SOUP   159
Elaine's Avgolemono Soup   160

KOTA KAPAMA: MY NEW TRADITIONAL
    BIRTHING MEAL   162
Angela's Kota Kapama   163

ROASTED CHESTNUTS   164
Angela's Roasted Chestnuts   165

MY FRENCH COUSIN   166
Gabrielle's Pilaf   167

HEALTHY OPTIONS   168
Elaine's Chicken and Turkey Tenders Kebabs   169
Kathryn's Meatless Eggplant Casserole   171

VII **The Baton Passes**   175

    LAMB BURGERS: THE NEXT GENERATION   175
      Noah's Lamb Burgers   176

    MY GRANDMOTHER'S SECRET COOKIE RECIPE   177

    ELENI'S COOKIES   180
      Angela's Melomacarona   181

Appendix A: Recipe Index   183
Appendix B: Cast of Characters   187
Appendix C: Glossary of Terms   191
Appendix D: Resources   193
Bibliography   195

Acknowledgements

Without the help of my family and friends, I couldn't have written and published this book. Their encouragement, memories, and recipes made this possible.

I could go back generations in acknowledging my family, but will limit myself to thank those who directly contributed to this book, especially my grandparents, Peter and Eleni Carlos and Stamatios and Despina Manolakas; my parents, Constantine and Angela Manolakas; my brother and his wife, Stanton and Barbara Manolakas; my aunts and uncles, Kathryn and Don Backos, Ginny and George Papageorge, George and Betty Manolakas, Lee and Chubby Manolakas, Gus and Ellen Carlos, Angelo Carlos, Bill Carlos; and my cousins: Sam, Perry, Dale, Sandy, Brian, Peachy, Gabrielle, Paul, George, Nick, Butch, Gigi, Bob, Stefan, and Stacy. I also include Aunt Tootsie and Uncle Nick Siokos, and Minnie Kirlakitsis, members of our extended family. I also would like to thank the Schmitz family, too, for their interest and enthusiasm for this project: Art, Dee, Dan, Carolyn, Jim, Connie, and all my nieces and nephews.

I want to thank my children, Charles Hawes and Sally Smith, my step-sons, Noah and Darshan Schmitz, and their wives and husband, Susan, Eric, Kim, and Azusa, for requesting, eating, and loving my Greek recipes. They also offered memories of their own and even one recipe. Most important, they have given me a fine bunch of grandchildren: Lila, Rubini, Asher, Maranatha, Isaac, Natasha, and Kai. My grandchildren were my inspiration and motivation for this book, because I believe in the importance of history, especially our own, and what it has to teach us. I wanted to share my family's history and Greek traditions with them.

There are so many friends who have supported me in this endeavor, they are too many to name. I would like to specify a few who were directly connected with this project: Penny Warner, my teacher and mentor; Constance Pike and Lani Longshore, my editors; and the members of the Tri-Valley branch of the California Writer's Club. I extend a special thanks to fellow members of the Institute of Transpersonal Psychology's Board of Trustees, Starlight Stitchers, and Soheila Habibian's belly dancing class, for being faithful tasters and reviewers of all the dishes I tested with them. I thank also the students of my Greek cooking classes. They have shared the love and fun of making Greek food with me.

Most of all, I'd like to thank my husband, Steven. It is a brave man who marries into a large Greek family. He has lent me courage and given me support in following my dreams to write, including photographing most of the food photos in this book. He has also helped me to connect with my ancestors, to gain their strength and guidance.

Introduction:
A Taste for Nostalgia

Have you ever sat down to eat one of your mother's signature meals, and with the first burst of flavor on your tongue you are magically transported to her kitchen, back in time and space to when you were a small child? Once again, you taste her delicious food, all wrapped in love and warmth. That's how it is with Greek food and me. Let's say I take a bite of stuffed tomatoes and green peppers; suddenly I am at our cottage in Canada. It is midsummer in the 1950s. The waves gently lap on the shore of Lake St. Clair, and the sounds of the cicadas crease the end of the day. Or I buy a bowl of rice pudding at a local Greek festival. With the first spoonful I am visiting my parents in Whittier, California, circa 1987, surrounded by my mother's treasured belongings, the pictures she painted, and her collection of fine antiques, listening to the constant background buzz of the TV.

Food can be like that. It not only makes me salivate, it also makes me remember. Its taste and smell trigger the neurons that tap deep into my memory, to a large bank of stories of my life and my family.

Three Carlos Cook, circa 1965: Left to right: Angela, Eleni, and Kathryn

It's with this dual effect of food in mind, sustenance for both the body and soul, that I created this book.

I owe a lot to my mother for any culinary successes I have had in my life and to my grandmothers and grandfathers and aunts, all the cooks in my family. They took the ancient formulas that were handed down to them—a pinch of this, a handful of that—and rendered the amounts into modern measurements. They modified their recipes as the years passed to make use of new laborsaving techniques, to please the modern palate, and to satisfy the need for healthier cooking. And from those time-honored recipes they made wonderful food.

My family is as distinctive and delightful as their cuisine, so they have also given me happy memories. In this book I share some of their stories along with their recipes.

To keep up with the changing times and culture, I have provided many options and substitutions to these traditional dishes. Those marked with the bullet symbol of ♥ provide healthier substitutions to the original ingredients. Whatever choices you make, I hope this book provides you with both nourishment and entertainment. I dedicate this book to my mother and her kitchen, and to all my other relatives whose food and recipes I have enjoyed. Good appetite, or as the Greeks would say, "*Kali Orexi!*"

Good appetite, or as the Greeks would say, "Kali Orexi!"

A FAMILY OF COOKS

My family immigrated to the United States from different parts of Greece early in the twentieth century, armed to the teeth with culinary talent and scrumptious recipes. My primary link to this lineage of luscious food was my mother, Angela Carlos Manolakas, who was an excellent cook. She had a knack of putting together just the right amounts of ingredients—be they olive oil, oregano or mint, lamb or chicken, tomatoes, green peppers, or onions—to come up with gustatory works of art. Her friends and family all sought after and enjoyed her food.

Angela grew up during the 1920s and 30s, in a family whose life revolved around cooking and feeding people. Not only did her mother, Eleni, cook for her husband and five children (Gus, Angela, Billy, Angelo, and Kathryn), she also fed a series of boarders who lived with the family in an upper flat, a house always crowded with guests. They lived on Macomb Street in Detroit, Michigan, in a neighborhood filled with other recent immigrants from all of Greece and its islands. Today the place is still known as Greektown and was distinguished by its many popular Greek restaurants and coffee houses. Angela's father, Peter Carlos, manned a small hamburger and snack shack he had built in front of their house next to the Greek church, the primary source of the family's income even through the Depression. The specialties of Peter's enterprise were his hamburgers and the cookies my grandmother baked from their secret recipe.

At the age of 22, my mother married into a family of restaurateurs when she wed my father, Constantine Manolakas. My father's parents, Stamatios and Despina Manolakas, owned and ran the Brown Cow Restaurant on the east side of Detroit, and his Uncle Mike owned the Neon Coney Island near downtown. My father had one sister, Ginny, and two brothers, George and Lee. Lee became the owner and manager of a series of restaurants including Brookfield's, a chain of coffee shops in the Sacramento, California area, now owned and operated by my cousins. On both sides of my family eating was their living, and they lived to eat.

~

(See Appendix B for a complete listing of the family.)

The Early Carlos Cooks

CHAPTER I

GLIEKO

Peter Kaloyeropoulos and his brother, whose name we have forgotten, left Kalamata for America before 1914. Eleni Foumaki and her sister, Mary, left the island of Crete shortly after, bound for the same destination. As the brothers came through the United States immigrant entry point an immigration officer shortened their long ethnic last name to Carlos. Peter and Eleni met and married in Detroit, Michigan, where they both had settled.

My grandparents had a fruitful and happy marriage. Peter's wife and children adored him as a caring and fun-loving man. However, I was appalled by the story my mother told me of their courtship.

My *yaya* (grandmother in Greek), a good-looking and educated young woman, was sought after by two men as soon as she arrived in this country—my *papou* (grandfather in Greek) and another suitor, who was from Crete. Because the Greeks of that time preferred to mix with and marry those from their own villages or islands, *Papou* was at a distinct disadvantage in his suit. To secure the prize of *Yaya*'s hand, he lied to her, announcing that he would have her deported if she didn't marry him. My mother laughed when she told me this anecdote, as if he had pulled a clever and harmless trick. Whatever Eleni's reasons, she decided to marry this bold, young man, and they lived a rich, full life together until he died in 1938.

I was appalled by the story my mother told me of their courtship.

The Carlos Family, 1934: Front, left to right, Kathryn and Bill; back, left to right, Angelo, Eleni, Peter, Gus, and Angela

When guests arrived,
they were fed a
spoonful of whole-fruit
marmalade and a glass
of fresh, cool water.

The convivial Carlos family lived in the house on Macomb Street through the early 1930s, with visiting and entertaining their primary pastimes. They dwelt in the midst of the Greek community's social whirl, and they relished it. My mother told me of the many parties they gave, typically after church on Sunday. Peter would sit at the head of his dining room table, dispensing homemade wine to his friends and family, while everybody around the table would tell stories of their *Patrida,* their villages in the old country, and sing songs. (The Carlos' were reputed for their beautiful voices and claimed to be cousins of Maria Callas.)

Eleni also entertained the ladies of the community throughout the week. In both cases, they welcomed their guests in the traditional Greek way, with *Glieko* (Spoon Sweets). When the guests arrived, they would be escorted to the table and fed a spoonful of whole-fruit marmalade and a glass of fresh, cool water.

When I was a young girl *Yaya* would serve us this treat on our weekly visits to her house. She must have been partial to grapefruit and kumquats spoon sweets, because she served them to us the most—tangy and sweet, and very sticky.

Fortunately, I inherited an unusual heirloom of this tradition from my mother, *Yaya* Eleni's silver-plated *glieko* server. It is shaped like a small loving cup, and around the top edge are twelve slots for teaspoons, enough for twelve guests. The server holds one cup of this simple treat.

The following recipe provides one of the many variations of the basic recipe that my grandmother served. Recipes for the other flavors she served, rose petal and kumquat, have been lost.

Eleni's Grapefruit Spoon Sweets—Glieko

Yields 48 grapefruit curls, about 8 8-oz. jars of preserve

6 whole thick-skinned grapefruit
3 cups sugar
3 cups water
1 oz. orange juice

Pieces of succulent, sweet grapefruit glieko to serve your guests

1. With a grater, grate off only the shiny, yellow part of the rind, leaving the white, dull surface underneath. Cut the fruit into 8 lengthwise wedges. Carefully remove the fruit from the rind to create 8 long wedge-shaped strips of rind. Roll up each strip and thread through with a darning needle and heavy-duty thread or string, to create a necklace of rolled rinds. Each necklace should hold 10–12 rolled rinds.

2. Place the rolled and threaded rinds in a large pan of fresh water and boil for 30 minutes, until tender. Drain.

3. Repeat step 2, but only until water reaches the boiling point. Drain again and repeat a third time. Drain and leave in fresh water overnight. (Steps 2 and 3 remove the bitterness from the rind.)

4. The next day, drain the water and place the rind rolls on paper toweling to dry.

5. Boil the sugar, water, and orange juice together until syrup is ready. To test syrup: Dip a spoon in syrup, and allow it to drip onto a plate. If the last drop remains on the spoon like a small bead and will not drip, the spoon sweet is ready.

Continued on next page

6. Carefully remove the strings from the necklaces of rolled rinds and place the fruit in the syrup. Simmer for 5 minutes. Remove pan from heat and let stand covered for 1 day.

7. Preserving instructions: After the sweet is prepared, fill hot, sterilized half-pint canning jars with the preparation, leaving 1/4 inch space at the top. Wipe jars and jar-threads clean, and place hot, sterilized lids on jars, screwing bands on firmly. Place on a rack in a deep pan of boiling water. (Water should be deep enough to cover jars at least 1 inch over the top). A canning pot would be helpful, but not necessary. Boil for 5 minutes. Remove immediately and place 2–3 inches apart on a cooling rack that has been covered by several layers of cloth. Keep out of drafts.

OPTION

♥ Substitute agave for sugar: Use 2 cups of water and 3 cups agave for the recipe. The resulting glieko will be just as sweet, but the syrup may be thinner than the sugar syrup.

PETER CARLOS' SNACK SHACK BURGERS

The women in my family have influenced my cooking the most— passing on to me the majority of recipes and stories in this book. They were the ones in our family who prepared and served the food on a daily basis, and they also lived long enough to tell me their tales. I would be remiss, however, if I said nothing about the men. We were Greeks after all, and true to the stereotype of that generation, the men owned restaurants.

Peter Carlos, my mother's father, started a food stand in front of his house in Greektown Detroit, next to the Annunciation Greek Church and Greek School. He built it himself from scrap wood, making it large enough to house a grill and sturdy enough to withstand the cold Detroit winters. Only a small part of this once vital neighborhood still exists in modern downtown Detroit. My mother's house, across the street from the church, was torn down around 1960 to make way for a large parking garage. A large, stately Greek Cathedral, the seat of the archdiocese of Detroit, has replaced the Greek Church. A large city block of Greektown adjacent to the cathedral was demolished in order to build first tourist shops and then the busy, modern Greektown Casino. But nearby Monroe Street, crowded and colorful with its old Greek restaurants and cafes, still survives.

Late in the last century, I visited this neighborhood and shared a late night dinner with my Aunt Kathryn and her family at the *Laikon Café*. Laikon means "people's place" in Greek. It has been in business since the 1920s, just after my grandfather established his snack shack. My relatives and I ate fried *Calamari*, crisp Greek salads, *pastitsio*, and roasted chicken oregano and potatoes, leaving room for a dessert of *baklava*. Even at 10:00 P.M., the dining room was crowded with loquacious, voracious patrons, including the august presence of the Metropolitan, (a Greek Orthodox head bishop) of the Detroit area. As small as Greektown has become, I could still feel the vibrancy and energy of those early years during that visit.

From his shack my grandfather sold fresh fruit, penny candy, and Greek sweets like *loukoumi* and *halvah*, roasted chestnuts, hamburgers, and our family's legendary cookies to the school children, church congregation, and many of the neighbors. Every weekend *Papou* would take his children to the large, open-air Eastern Market in downtown Detroit to purchase the fresh grapes, pears, apples, and walnuts, almonds, chestnuts, and pistachios he would sell the following week. *Yaya* baked a steady supply of their cookies, which customers loved to dunk into cups of strong, steamy coffee, and *Papou* cooked his hamburgers on a compact grill in the stand. He never

Yaya baked a steady supply of their cookies; Papou cooked his hamburgers on a compact grill.

PETER CARLOS' SNACK SHACK HAMBURGERS

Yields 3–4 hamburgers

1 lb. ground beef
¼ cup chopped onions
2–3 slices day old sweet French or Italian
    bread, torn into very small pieces
Salt and pepper to taste
1 egg, beaten (optional)

1. Mix the ingredients in a bowl until thoroughly blended (using clean hands works best). Shape the meat into patties about 3 inches in diameter and about ½–¾ inch thick.

2. Fry on a greased grill or griddle, medium to medium-well.

OPTIONS

- Use ground buffalo or turkey meat instead of beef.
- Broil or barbecue the burgers, medium to medium well done.
- Add a splash of wine: Sauvignon Blanc for turkey, Zinfandel for the red meats.
- Add ¼–½ tsp. garlic granules.
- Add ¼ cup Feta cheese, finely crumbled.

became wealthy through the business, but he provided for his large family, even through the Great Depression.

When I was small my mother used to make hamburgers for our family using his recipe. They were juicy, flavorful, and old-fashioned. My brother Stan, who fancied himself an authority on hamburgers, favored the modern American version—straight ground beef, pressed no more than ½ inch flat, grilled quickly, and smothered in mustard and ketchup. To please his palate my mother made us the modern patties, and my grandfather's burgers fell out of favor at our house. Only occasionally would my mother make them to satisfy her nostalgic taste for her bygone home. Today this burger of humble origins, with its beefy proportions and added ingredients, would be touted as a gourmet hamburger.

AND THEY HAULED PETER OFF TO JAIL

The following events happened in the summer of 1924, during the time of Prohibition. My grandparents' neighborhood in Detroit teemed with newly arrived immigrants from all areas of Greece. Most people who lived there were poor; any extra money they earned they typically sent to family in the old country. Many were bachelors or husbands who had left their wives and children behind until the men could afford their passages. Every night these mustachioed men sat in the small brick coffeehouses that lined Monroe Street, shops with bright neon signs in the foreign Greek alphabet flashing names like The New Athens Café. They would sip their demitasse cups of coffee, fondle their worry beads, and heatedly argue the Greek political issues of the day. They were earnest and energetic people, but some of them skirted the law to make their way in a new land.

When my grandparents, Peter and Eleni, lived just off of Monroe on the top floor of a flat on Macomb Street, the bottom floor was occupied by another family—a man and his wife, his mother, and his two brothers. They were an unruly bunch from a different part of Greece and not numbered among my grandparents' friends. Early one day, three policemen walked around to the back of this house. Out her kitchen window Eleni noticed them looking at a sheet of paper and then up at the upper flat. They seemed to be looking for an address, but no numbers were marked on either story. The men looked back at the paper, discussing something. Then Eleni heard them running up the stairs to her small back porch. They stood there between Peter's many potted plants, including a large potted pear tree, before the officers started pounding on the back door with their fists and Billy clubs. Alerted by the noise, Peter ran into the kitchen and opened the door. He hurried out to see what they wanted, while Eleni cowered in the kitchen, peeking through the curtains. She saw the three cops nab him, knocking over some of the pots in the disturbance, and even though Peter was a stout, strong man, they easily pulled him down the stairs into the backyard.

The police were yelling something at him that neither Peter nor Eleni could understand, since they knew very little English. They were confused and scared by the sudden commotion, neither of them comprehending what was happening. For hundreds of years a visit from the authorities in Greece would have meant that the governing Turks were there to either conscript the men into their army or put them in prison for insurrection.

Since my nine-year-old Uncle Gus and my seven-year-old mother were the only ones in the family who spoke English, Eleni commanded them to accompany her and confront the policemen. Screaming and crying, she ran down the stairs behind them. The three comprised an unlikely force to confront the law. Eleni, even at her full height, was less than five feet tall, and her children were spunky but short and skinny. While Peter, pitched forward on the ground by the cops' rough treatment, was being handcuffed, Eleni screamed at the children in Greek, "You, *morae* (morons)! Do something!! Don't let them take him away. They're *policia*! They're Turks! We'll never see your *patera* (father) again!" My uncle and mother could only stand there—eyes big and round, mouths gaping, lips trembling. They were too young and sheltered to know what the words "Prohibition" and "arrest" and "bootlegging" meant, the words the officers were using.

As Eleni continued to exhort them, my mother and uncle finally grabbed Peter around the waist and legs, trying to pull him from the clutches of the lawmen. By now the children were also screaming and crying, fearful that Peter Carlos would be taken away from them forever.

The police shook the children off and left with my grandfather, his head hanging as they dragged him across the yard. They threw him into the back of an old, black paddy wagon, and the family was left in the yard, dazed—with Eleni crying and wringing her hands.

The rest of the day and evening was terrible for the family, as they sat inside the house, not knowing why Peter had been arrested and what his fate would be. At dinner Eleni sat with her young children praying to the large icon of *Panagia* (Mary) and the Christ Child that her husband would be delivered from his plight. She tried to comfort the children as they slowly ate their dinner of Greek bread, olives, lamb and potatoes, with a pot of cooked dandelions. Taking out her handkerchief to wipe away her tears, she said, "Tomorrow we will talk to the *Papa* (priest). He will know what to do."

Early the next morning as they prepared to visit the priest, the paddy wagon pulled up again. My grandmother tightly held her children and watched from her high window as one of the policemen exited the wagon and opened its back door. My grandfather climbed out, his clothes wrinkled and disheveled. The policeman clapped him on the back and shook his hand. My grandfather surreptitiously wiped his hand on his pants and started walking to the back door.

As that was happening, several other policemen poured out of a police car. Some ran to the back door of the lower flat while others rushed around the house to the front door. They beat on the back door, and when nobody answered, two of them lowered their shoulders and broke it down. They disappeared momentarily into the house and then came back out leading the three real bootleggers, the man and his brothers who lived in the bottom flat. The cops threw them into the

My mother and uncle grabbed Peter around the waist and legs to pull him from the clutches of the lawmen.

paddy wagon, as other cops came out of the house carrying the still for making bathtub gin.

Peter's family watched from the window as he swiftly climbed the back stairs and came into the flat. He put his arms out to hug them. They ran into his arms as they all laughed and kissed each other in joy and relief. Peter explained, "I finally understood that they were looking for bootleggers, and then I had to explain to them that the neighbors below were the bootleggers. The *policia* came to the wrong home." My guess is that they celebrated his release with a big party, which would have included many friends and a bottle of homemade wine that my grandfather continued to make legally in his bathtub for his own use.

The Greeks have been wine connoisseurs since ancient times, when Dionysus was the Greek god of wine. With the hot, dry Mediterranean climate and mountainous geography, Greece has always had the environment to be a major wine producer. A widely known white wine is Retsina, a traditional mixture of the white savatiano grape and the resin from the Aleppo pine forests of Attica. The Retsina of my grandfather's time had a harsh, resinous taste; however, modern blends can be milder, more earthy than pungent. I recently tried a Retsina from Thessalonika, produced by Malamatinas, exceptional for its clarity of flavors and smooth finish.

See Appendix D for a resource list of two informative websites that feature modern Greek wines.

Standard Rosés include Roditys and Kokineli, a resin-flavored red. Traditional dessert wines include Mavrodaphne and Muscat, which has been a famous product for centuries from the island of Samos. Brandies include Metaxa and Masticha, which is anise-flavored. A more notorious anise-flavored intoxicant from Greece is Ouzo, a wonderful, yet powerful cocktail, which can be drunk straight in thimble-sized glasses or with water or ice.

15 year-old Angela in Cretan costume, 1932

The Mediterranean villa was surrounded by flocks of sheep and the sweet smell of oregano and basil.

CRETAN COOKING

Because *Yaya* Eleni Carlos was born in Crete, I have always nursed a fascination for that island. In school I learned about the mythical labyrinth and the advanced Minoan civilization. I heard amazing tales of my grandmother's childhood in Chania, which were validated when I watched the movie, Zorba the Greek. I thought of it as a primitive place, albeit beautiful and magical. When my husband, Steven, and I visited the island, I was awed by Crete's beauty and ancient culture.

We stayed in a palatial villa on the edge of the Mediterranean, surrounded by pastures populated with flocks of sheep and sweet with the smell of oregano, basil, and other wild herbs and flowers. The shepherds held classic crooks in their hands as they whistled signals to their sheep dogs, which were running around the flocks to herd them together. Abandoned ruins more than 7000 years old lay within modern cities crowded by tourists. One day we drove through a resort where we could have gone skiing in the snow-covered White Mountains in the morning and then taken a dip in the nearby Mediterranean in the afternoon.

One day, after we ate lunch at the seaside town of Aghios Nicholaos, with its calm blue bay studded with colorful fishing boats, we traveled to a nearby mountain village. As we entered the village's one-block shopping district, an old-world funeral procession wound its way down the main street, not much wider than the compact car we had rented. Unable to back up or turn around, we were forced to pull up on the narrow sidewalk to make room for the procession. Two priests, dressed in rich red ceremonial robes, led it swinging their censors of incense. Altar boys followed them and then a cadre of old women dressed in black. The women were professional mourners who howled and beat their chests. Behind them walked the grieving family and the stately pallbearers carrying the coffin. The end of this parade was signaled by young women with basketsful of bagged peanuts that they threw to the

Eleni's Kallitsounakia

Yields 36–40 cookies

Preheat oven 400 degrees

Dough

4 cups flour
½ tsp. salt
¼ cup sugar
½ lb. butter
1 egg
½ cup milk

Filling

¾ lb. shelled almonds, coarsely
    chopped
3 slices of wheat rusks or zwieback
¾ cup sugar
½ tsp. cloves
½ tsp. cinnamon
½ tsp. almond extract (optional)
¼–⅓ cup honey

Topping

Powdered sugar
Rosewater (optional)

Kallitsounakia: Tiny pie with a honey-nut filling

1. Make the filling by moistening the rusks or zwieback and mashing it into the chopped nuts and sugar until well mixed. Add the spices, then enough honey to bind the mixture together.
2. To make pastry dough, sift flour with salt and sugar; cut in butter with a pastry cutter or 2 knives.

Continued on next page

3. Mix egg and milk together. Using a fork, blend this liquid into the flour and butter mixture.

4. Roll or pat out walnut-size pieces of dough into circles about 3½ inches in diameter. Put a rounded tablespoon of filling in the center of the circle and close the dough over the filling. (This can be done in several creative ways, such as, fold it over into a half-circle and press the edges together with a fork or pinch the sides up to form a basket with a narrow opening.)

5. Place on a cookie sheet and bake in a 400-degree oven for 20 minutes.

6. Sprinkle cooled pieces with rosewater (optional) and dust with powdered sugar.

NOTE

Wheat rusks are a Greek specialty food item. See Appendix D, Resources for ordering information.

OPTION

Use half almonds, half walnuts.

onlookers. The peanuts were a local variation of the Greek tradition of *kollyva*, a plate of boiled wheat symbolizing everlasting life and hope, which is distributed during funerals and memorial services.

Our last day on the island we visited Knossos, the beautiful and mysterious center of the Minoan empire. The site was purchased and restored by English archeologist Robert Evans in 1900, in part to educate the modern visitor on the sophisticated and technologically advanced civilization that thrived from 3000 to 1500 BC. Throughout the time we knocked around the ruins I wondered how my grandmother could leave such an enchanted place. The economic and political conditions around the time of the island's independence from Turkish domination in 1909 must have been dire, and the allure of the New World irresistible, to woo Eleni from her fabled homeland.

Before we left I purchased an island cookbook: *Cretan Cooking: The Miracle of the Cretan Diet*, by Maria and N. Psilakis, circa 1995. It introduced me to the rich variety of foods the resourceful people from this island created from everything edible they could find. They cooked every part of the animals they raised, indigenous plants garnered from the fields, snails, and the many varieties of edible creatures they fished from the sea.

My grandmother left some of the recipes back in the old country. Thank goodness! Octopus, which I'm not personally keen on, is featured in many of the seafood offerings. A gelatin mold from pigs' heads and feet is also listed in the book. And there's the "delicacy to be found all over Crete," consisting only of spleen and intestines (I'm assuming lamb), seasoned by salt, lemon, and pepper. What she did import were her family's versions of the classics: *spanakopita* (a cheese and spinach pie made with phyllo pastry), stuffed vegetables, roast lamb, breads, and traditional desserts.

I discovered one very old recipe in my Yaya's collection for *kallitsounakia,* which I remember her moistening the zwieback needed for its crust. From the book, I learned it was rooted in Cretan cuisine as an Easter delicacy, like the *kallitsounia* recipes I found listed. However, it differed from them in that it resembles more of a cookie than a sweet cheese pie. To me this confection is quaint and old-fashioned and absolutely delicious.

The Early
Manolakas Clan

The Manolakas side of my family emigrated from the island of Chios, which stands about five miles off the coast of Turkey. The Manolakas' were seafarers from the little village of Langada. In Greece my *papou*, Sam Manolakas, was a sea captain when he was twenty. My grandmother, *Yaya* Despina, was raised in the outskirts of the island's capital, the city of Chios, where her father (my maternal great-grandfather) Elias Vlisides was a teacher and a Greek Orthodox priest.

Since Chios was under Turkish domination until 1913, many Greek men fled the island to avoid conscription into the Turkish army. For this reason, Sam, his fiancée Despina, and her five brothers came to America in 1912, originally settling in Massachusetts. Soon after Sam and Despina's marriage, the entire family moved to Detroit to work in the infant auto industry. Except for a two-year return to the old country when my father, Constantine, was in his early teens, Sam and Despina worked and raised their family in Detroit's Greek community.

LOUKOUMADES

When I knew my *Yaya* Despina, she was a formidable woman at five-feet-six by 225 pounds, the epitome of the family matriarch.

The Manolakas' were seafarers from the village of Langada, where my grandfather, Sam, was a sea captain at twenty.

My father's origins:
Langada, Chios, Greece

She wore widow's weeds over the big ledge of her chest and stomach from the time she was 55, when a neighbor accidentally ran over my grandfather with a car in front of their house and killed him. *Yaya* had dark, expressive arched eyebrows and a wide grin of perfectly even false teeth. Her silver-gray hair was pulled tightly into a bun, held together by at least two-dozen silver hairpins. I loved it when, as a child, she let me comb her long, straight hair with a silver backed comb before she braided and rolled it into place.

Yaya had two acclaimed dessert recipes: *Loukou-mades* or Honey Balls, as our family called them, and Paximadia. When she fried up the *Loukoumades* she did so as a feast for a crowd. Most often the party would take place at the summer cottage she shared with her daughter, Ginny, and son-in-law, George, which was next door to my parent's cottage on Lake St. Claire in Ontario, Canada. The small place would be packed with gregarious relatives—my aunts, uncles, and cousins. After dinner and before the adults began their long evening of playing pinochle or canasta, *Yaya* would uncover the dough that had been rising in her kitchen that afternoon and begin frying up dozens of these Greek fritters.

The Manolakas family 1929: Front, left to right, Elias, Despina, Eugenia; back left to right, George, Constantine, Stamatios

The secret of her success with this delicacy was one Greek word—*koufia*, or fluffy. When she passed her tricks on to her grandson, Nicky, she emphasized, "*Koufia! Koufia, Nikaki!*" She would sink her hands into the large pan of elastic and liquid-like dough in front of her, calmly squeezing it up past her curled thumb and index finger into walnut-sized bubbles. She would then scrape off the bubble with a spoon and drop it into a large cauldron of hot oil. *Yaya* would spoon, turn, and retrieve these bobbing blobs for what seemed like hours. When they had cooked into golden brown balls, she'd scoop them out with a slotted spoon, drain them on paper towels, and dump them, still warm, into bowls. All the while the family waited impatiently, salivating for their servings of this much-loved treat. We would pour her warm honey-flavored syrup over our mounds of balls, sprinkle them with cinnamon, and proceed to stuff them whole, one at a time, into our mouths.

My teeth would pierce the hot, crunchy shell of each ball into the soft gooey dough inside. The honeyed syrup, accented with rich spice and meaty chopped nuts, bathed the balls with its sweet flavor. This

DESPINA'S LOUKOUMADES—HONEY BALLS

Yields 4½ dozen

3 pkgs. dry yeast
3 lbs. flour
I tsp. salt
I egg
I cup milk
4½ cups lukewarm to warm water
Vegetable oil for frying

SYRUP

2 cups sugar
1¼ cups water
½ cup honey

Loukoumades: Soaked in syrup, dusted with nuts and cinnamon

1. Add yeast to I cup warm water. Stir until completely dissolved.
2. In a large bowl or pan mix the 3 pounds of flour with I teaspoon salt.
3. Combine milk and sugar and stir in dissolved yeast until well mixed.
4. Mix the yeast solution into the dry ingredients with your hand.
5. Beat the egg into the other liquids, and then add to the flour mixture. Mix in with your hand.
6. Squeeze and knead the mixture as you slowly add the other 3 cups of warm water. (Dredge your hands with flour and keep them coated, to ensure the dough does not stick to you hands as you knead it.) Mix all the water in. (The more water the fluffier the mix—the right amount will be fined tuned with experience. Try for a light, spongy consistency.)
7. Sprinkle flour on top of the mixture. Put a dishtowel over the bowl, and

Continued on next page

then cover with a blanket to keep warm. Let it rise 2–3 hours or until the dough has doubled in size.

8. After it rises add more water, beating it with your hand, until you can squeeze the liquefied dough through your hand into a bubble at the top of your fist (through the circle of the thumb and forefinger). The description of the consistency at this point is "not runny but not cakey." If, as you cook it, the dough seems to be too thick or cakey, add a little water until the proper consistency is reached.

9. Pull the dough and squeeze it through your hand into the circle described in step 8 above. Scoop the dough ball off your hand with a tablespoon and plop it into oil, preheated to 350 degrees in a heavy Dutch oven or large soup kettle. Oil should be at least 2 inches deep.

10. Turn the frying dough balls over when edges show color, frying until they are a uniform golden brown. (The test of your mixture will be that you will produce balls that are spongy with hollow spaces in the center.) Drain on absorbent paper.

11. To make the syrup, put its ingredients into a saucepan and bring to a boil. Simmer for 10 minutes. Cool until just warm.

12. For each serving put several balls in a bowl and douse with syrup. Sprinkle with cinnamon and/ or chopped nuts.

Bet you can't eat just one bowl!

perfect blend of taste and texture was irresistible to me. One bowl was never enough.

I don't remember her ever eating any of them; she was too busy cooking. And, in my estimation, she never made them enough times. I could have eaten them once a week, at least.

When she died I thought the recipe had died with her. However, one Thanksgiving my cousin Nicky, whom she had personally raised, surprised us all by making them. Sometime in his youth she had trained him in this art of squeezing, scooping, plopping, turning, and retrieving. Even though I was full of holiday dinner that year, I passed

My teeth pierced the ball's hot, crunchy shell to the soft gooey dough inside. The sweet flavor of the honeyed syrup bathed it. One bowl was never enough.

on the pumpkin pie and grabbed a bowl of my cousin's unexpected gift. The balls were delicious, and once again, like long ago, I was sitting at the table, surrounded by my vociferous and voracious cousins eating *Loukoumades*. By now they were all successful and seasoned professionals—lawyers, doctors, and teachers. But at that moment we were all Despina's grandkids, stuffing ourselves with this delectable treat.

PAXIMADIA

Yaya Despina baked her *Paximadia*, the Greek version of Italian biscotti or German zwieback, for us to eat on a daily basis—no fanfare or feast, just cookies in the jar. She initially baked the cookie in a long three-inch hump of dough that she sliced at one-half inch intervals most of the way through. After this initial baking, she took it from the oven so she could finish slicing the pieces, then laid them on their sides and baked them first on one side and then the other. The result was a crunchy, crisp cookie, which we dunked in coffee or cocoa.

Traditionally, *paximadia* are served after funerals at the *makaria* (the traditional meal to bless the dearly departed), "because they are dry, like bones, and not too sweet." (From *A Guide to Greek Traditions and Customs in America*, by Marilyn Rouvelas.)

Since a cookie too sweet would be considered celebratory, this one is deemed the most suitable. I have attended many Greek *makaria* where I was greeted at the door with this traditional offering and a thimbleful of Metaxa, a Greek brandy. After the travail of the funeral, they both have restored me, warming and filling me with food, spirits, and a renewed appreciation for life.

My introduction to *paximadia* was more happily associated with visits to *Yaya* Despina's house. (Though she lived with Aunt Ginny, Uncle George, and cousin Nicky from the time I was born to her death 27 years later, we always referred to their house as *Yaya* Despina's.) The adults sat in the big kitchen for café (coffee and dessert), while

Despina's Paximadia

Yields approximately 50 cookies

Preheat oven to 375 degrees

Cookie dough

¼ lb. butter
⅛ tsp. baking soda, dissolved with
    ½ tsp. orange juice
½ cup shortening
½ cup orange juice
1⅙ cups sugar
1 rind of orange, freshly grated
3 eggs
⅛ cup (or ½–¾ jigger) whiskey or
    brandy
5¼ to 6 cups flour
2 tbsp. + ½ tsp. of baking powder

Filling

2 tsp. Cinnamon
1 tbsp. sugar
10 walnuts or pecans, chopped

Paximadia: Twice baked, great for dunking in coffee

1. Cream together butter and shortening; then cream in sugar.
2. Add eggs, baking soda, orange juice, orange rind, and whiskey or brandy. Mix after each addition.
3. Mix baking powder with flour and sift and fold into the other ingredients a couple of cups at a time. The dough will get too thick to stir. Knead in the flour at that point with your hand.

Continued on next page

Continue to knead the dough until it is smooth and elastic. It will be ready when it no longer sticks to your fingers.

4. Roll out dough in a sausage shape, approximately 3" x 12" (or the length of your cookie sheet); even the edges and flatten the surface to about ½" thick. Put the filling in a ½" line down the middle of the flattened dough.

5. Fold over and slice crosswise, but not all the way through, into ¾ inch slices. Bake ½ hour, or until lightly brown, in an oven set at 375 degrees, then lower the oven temperature to 350 degrees.

6. Take the cookies from the oven and cut through the roll. Lay the resulting pieces on their sides and brown in the oven.

7. Turn over and brown on the other side. Browning the cookies on both sides should take 20–30 more minutes.

OPTION

You can use this dough to make koulourakia, as my grandmother did. Instead of making the dough into the long sausage described in step 4, use it to form the traditional koulourakia shapes (see any other koulourakia recipe in this book for that information). Bake in a 375-degree oven for 30–35 minutes.

My grandmother's unique recipe added a filling of cinnamon, sugar, and chopped nuts she spooned down the middle of the length of dough

the kids took their plates and stole away either to watch Bonanza or Mitch Miller on TV or to listen to the latest hits on Nicky's phonograph. At that time we were big Perry Como fans. On many occasions the featured dessert was my grandmother's unique recipe for this cookie, distinguished from many others by the addition of a filling of cinnamon, sugar, and chopped nuts she spooned down the middle of the length of dough, before it was folded over to make the characteristic hump.

This made hers a little sweeter than the funereal version, and with a little more spice and crunch. They taste delicious and stay fresh a long time.

My mother and father loved them, and many years later, after Despina had died, my mother became the *paximadia* baker, making huge batches to share with family and friends. She also treated her coworkers at the East Whittier City School District office with these offerings from her Greek kitchen. They were a hit with everybody.

SAM MANOLAKAS' FLY TRAP

Sam Manolakas, my father's father, started his restaurant career by owning a food stand in Dearborn, Michigan, outside the River Rouge Ford Plant where he had once worked. Selling lunches and snacks to the factory workers, he made enough money to start his restaurant, The Brown Cow, on the east side of Detroit. (I have never able to find out why they called it that. It is certain they never owned a cow.) The restaurant became a fixture in its neighborhood and was a commercial success—selling great food at reasonable prices and providing fast and friendly service. Sadly, the menus and recipes for the meals cooked and served at the restaurant have been lost, but fortunately, however, the story about Sam's fly trap was not.

Papou died before I was born, killed in an auto accident outside his home one snowy day during the winter of 1945, so I only know him by the few stories that my parents told me and by old photographs and home movies. My favorite story that I was told as a child was how much my grandfather would have loved me, and how he would have given me lots of money if I would have played the piano for him or spoken Greek to him or did well at school. After I had grown up, my father told me this story of how Sam was always trying to invent a better fly trap. It has become my new favorite story about my grandfather.

Sam had problems with flies at his restaurant. He owned The Brown Cow in the days long before air conditioning. Today we forget, if we ever knew, what life was like without air conditioning. In Detroit, it meant battling hot, muggy summers. Imagine how hot and stuffy the restaurant would be with its grill and ovens operating. So the doors were open during business hours from June through

Sam invented new fly traps constantly. Maybe this was what people did before TV, with only the technology of their own imagination.

Stamatia, past 90 years-old, and
Connie, mid-1980s

September, the restaurant presenting a smörgåsbord of flavors to the local fly population.

According to my dad, Sam tried new variations of fly traps constantly, like the proverbial fellow who sought to build a better mousetrap. Maybe inventing things was what many people did before the advent of television, when all they had was the technology of their own imagination.

What was there for a man to do at the end of the day, after he had finished work and reading the Greek-American newspaper all the way through? Sam would sit at home in his rocking chair, just outside the kitchen by the back door, smoking cigarettes (the only place Despina would allow him to smoke in the house). As he sat there he imagined ways to build traps to catch those pesky flies.

The trap my father remembered best was an elaborate structure resembling a beehive made of iron barbed wire, with ripe bananas placed inside as the bait. The wire wrapped from top to bottom, wire spikes along its length all facing into and down toward the bottom of the trap. The spikes bristled very close together, in order to trap the flies inside. The fly would enter the top, seduced by the strong, redolent smell of the ripe banana at the bottom, and wind its way down through the trap. It could make it to the banana, but it could not fly out without impaling its carcass on the spikes. So the fly and its fellows were doomed to buzz above the succulent, sweet bait until they died. I guess if you were a fly it was a great way to go.

VISITING MY OLD AUNTIE

Uncle Mike was my grandfather's younger brother. I knew and loved my uncle throughout my childhood. A restaurant owner, too, Mike operated The Neon Coney Island, a hamburger joint and grill in downtown Detroit. When I was a young child, my parents would take my brother, Stan, and I to visit him there at least once a month and to chow down on hamburgers and French fries. It was a small diner with a counter of maybe 15 swivel seats and another 15 dark green leather booths. A large smoky grill stood along the wall behind the counter, large fryers by its side. He would meet us at the door of the diner, dressed in a clean white shirt, gray pants, scuffed black shoes, and a paper fry-cook's hat perched on his bald head. Even though Uncle Mike was thin, he had to squeeze into "our" little booth to visit with us while we ate.

My brother, as a self-proclaimed expert on hamburgers, would only order that entree at restaurants during his childhood, comparing this favorite American dish across the country. He unequivocally voted Uncle Mike's the best hamburger he ever ate. I didn't care; I was there for the fries.

Uncle Mike's wife was *Thea* Stamatia. (*Thea* is aunt in Greek.) We called Mike "Uncle," but she was always "*Thea*" to my parents, my brother, and me. *Thea* Stamatia was a wonderful lady, sweet and energetic, and very hospitable. *Thea* and her sister, who lived with them, were even shorter than *Yaya* Eleni, perhaps 4 feet 8 inches— perhaps. They would meet us at the front door of their home dressed in fancy housedresses and black-laced shoes with chunky heels. Over her dress, *Thea* wore a crisp white apron while she cooked. Her sister wore her hair in soft, graying curls around her face, while Stamatia sported a neat bun.

The last time I saw her, when I was a grown woman with teenage children, she looked the same as ever. She was very interested in hearing about my daughter, Sally, who was sixteen at the time. She wanted to match-make her with a bachelor in his mid to late thirties whom she knew in Greece. "No *Thea*, that's okay. She's not interested in marriage yet," I said, calling her off my innocent daughter. And she lied to us about her age during the visit. She pretended she was in her eighties, no more than 85. But her younger cousin protested, reminding her she was at least 93.

She pretended she was no more than eighty-five. But her cousin reminded her she was at least ninety-three.

Stamatia's Koulourakia

Yields 36–40 varied shapes

Preheat oven to 350 degrees

1 cup softened butter
1 cup + 2 tbsp. sugar
1 jigger warm water
5 egg yolks (save egg whites for glaze)
1 jigger of whiskey
4 cups white flour (approximate)
¼ tsp. powdered cloves
1½ tbsp. baking powder
Finely chopped walnuts

A traditional favorite when guests come to visit

1. Cream butter; add sugar, and cream until light.
2. Add the water, egg yolks, and whiskey, and beat well.
3. Sift together the flour, cloves, and baking powder. Add the dry ingredients gradually to the creamed mixture. Add enough flour until the dough is smooth and pliable and does not stick to the bowl.
4. Roll into various lengths, about ¾ inch in diameter, and then form into different *koulourakia* shapes: e.g. circles, 3-inch lengths, 6-inch lengths doubled lengthwise, 6-inch lengths doubled lengthwise and twisted into a simple braid, spirals. (Use about 2–3 tbsp. of dough to form each of the shapes.)
5. Beat egg whites lightly. Brush the *koulourakia* shapes with the slightly beaten egg whites and then sprinkle with chopped nuts.
6. Bake for 25–30 minutes on a greased cookie sheet. Cool.

As children, my brother and I loved to visit *Thea*, but with trepidation. She liked to greet children by pinching their cheeks. In anticipation of that ritual, I would meet her with more of a grimace than a smile on my face, which would unfortunately cause my cheeks to pooch up into very pinchable shapes. She just couldn't resist. Squeezing them tightly in her tiny but strong fingers, she moved my cheeks back and forth, squealing in her uniquely high, squeaky voice. (*Thea*'s voice sounded like Joe Pesci on estrogen.) She would say to me, "*O, to koritsi!*" (Oh, you cute little girl.) Oh, the pain—I'd yelp and dance around and rub my cheeks when she let go, but I always let her do it. I loved her that much.

Then she would invite us into her crowded little dining room. The table was covered by a long, white lace tablecloth and set with her best china and silverware. She'd ask my father if he wanted a little *bifsteki*, steak, and regardless of his response (which in my father's case was usually yes), she would disappear into her kitchen to fry up one for him. Then she would load the table with desserts: *glieko, loukoumi, baklava,* almond milk, and Greek cookies, typically *kourembiedes* and *koulourakia*. All were very good.

It didn't matter if we had just eaten lunch before we got there; we were urged to eat, eat, eat, and as we ate the grown-ups would talk, all in Greek—*Thea* in her high, squeaky voice. When we finally pushed away from the table and left, we were stuffed with goodies and *Thea*'s love.

THE YAYA WARS

Both of my grandmothers were widowed for 30 years. According to Greek custom, this meant they were to remain unmarried for the rest of their days—wearing plain black dresses and dedicating their lives to their children and grandchildren. Both of my *yayas* were excellent examples of this tradition. *Yaya* Despina virtually raised my cousin

Thea couldn't resist pinching our cheeks as she greeted us with her high, squeaky voice.

The Carlos Cooks in 1965: left to right Elaine, Kathryn, Yaya Eleni, Angela; the men, left to right Cousin Brian, Connie, Bill

Nicky, while her daughter, Ginny, taught school. She also supplied a fair amount of babysitting to the rest of her eleven grandchildren. *Yaya* Eleni lived with my Uncle Bill, a quiet gentleman and perennial bachelor whose hair had traveled south by the time he was thirty, leaving him with a bald pate and the hairiest torso and legs I've ever seen on a man. She took care of my cousins, Sandy and Brian, after school, while her daughter, Kathryn, worked as a secretary. My grandmothers' primary form of recreation, as long as I knew them, was cooking for their families.

Each had their specialties. *Yaya* Despina was renowned for her *keftaides* (cocktail meatballs), *paximadia* (cookies), and *theples* and *loukoumades* (deep-fried confections). *Yaya* Eleni was the pastry chef, a legend for her secret cookie recipe and the rest of her desserts. It was over these pastries that I came to think of their relationship as "the *Yaya* wars."

These two very different females spent most of their holidays together for at least 12 years. They would sit in each other's company at these gatherings like wallflowers at a dance. They would wear their fanciest black widows' weeds, which included small hats with delicate decorative veils perched on their heads. Their feet, shod in their old-lady laced-up heels, would be primly crossed at the ankles.

Yaya Despina was big, round, and formidable. She had long, straight silver hair that she wound tightly into a bun. We thought of her as hale and hearty until she was well into her eighties. *Yaya* Eleni was short, round, and timid. Plagued by cataracts, she wore coke-bottle glasses to shore up her failing eyesight. What was left of her hair was cut short and permed, then collected under a thin hair net, presenting only a cloudy ghost of her thick, dark youthful mane. Her children constantly worried about the many physical ailments she suffered.

Yaya Despina spoke loudly in broken English and carried a big *koutala* (spoon), with which she would threaten her misbehaving

Yaya Despina in the 1950s

These two very different females would sit with each other at holiday gatherings like wallflowers at a dance.

They also came from different cooking traditions. Eleni Carlos used cinnamon in her meat dishes; Despina Manolakas eschewed the practice.

grandchildren, as in, "You stop hitting your sister, or I will bring out my big *koutala.*" *Yaya* Eleni spoke only Greek in a soft, reedy voice. She would discipline indirectly through suggestions to her children, as in "Angela, you better watch your daughter; she's sneaky."

They also came from different cooking traditions. Eleni Carlos used cinnamon in her meat dishes; Despina Manolakas eschewed the practice. Although they made the same traditional foods, they used different recipes with different spices and ingredients. Eleni used commercial phyllo for her pitas and desserts. Despina made her own phyllo. And every time they went head to head on a dessert, Eleni would win.

Every holiday they would show up at the same houses with their Easter bread or *Vasilopita* or *baklava* or *kolokithopita*. And each holiday people would have seconds of Eleni's offering, while Despina would need to urge people to try hers. I loved Yaya Eleni's dishes, but after I ate a big piece of the dessert she made I would loyally eat a big piece of Yaya Despina's offering, too. It was an act of love. Except for Despina's *theples, loukoumades* and *paximadia,* the rest of her pastries were, well . . . ho-hum.

Although Yaya Despina wasn't the best pastry cook in the family, she did very well with meat and potatoes and stews. I hankered for her *Keftaides,* spicy, oval meatballs that she served plain as appetizers or drenched in a rich tomato sauce over steaming hot spaghetti.

In this book I offer you the best of their dishes. Also, most of my mother's and Aunt Kathryn's recipes are derivatives of Eleni's as well. All are a testament to these two women's love of and devotion to their families. The next pages contain two from their collections.

DESPINA'S KEFTAIDES—GREEK MEAT BALLS

Yields 1½–2 dozen

1 lb. ground beef
½–¾ cup onion, minced
1–3 cloves garlic
½ tsp. salt
Dash pepper
2 tsp. dried oregano
2 tsp. dried mint
1–2 slices stale bread
½ cup dry red wine or water
1 large egg (optional)
Flour
Olive oil (optional)
Butter (optional)

1. Mix together meat, onion, garlic, salt, pepper, oregano, and mint.
2. Remove crusts from bread slices and moisten in wine or water. Add bread (shredded into pieces) and egg to meat.
3. Knead mixture. Shape into little ovals or torpedoes about 1½ inches long and about an inch wide at the middle.
4. Lightly coat with flour, and either sauté in equal amounts of olive oil and butter, or bake on an oiled cookie sheet at 350 degrees 20–30 minutes. Turn to brown evenly. Keep warm until served.

OPTIONS

- Use ground buffalo meat instead of ground beef.
- Stale bread can be white or wheat. Sweet French would be more authentic. The Greeks would use the crusts; you may or may not want to—your choice. If you use bread crumbs, use ½ cup and do not add the wine or water.
- If you use fresh herbs, use 2 tbsp. of oregano and 1 tbsp. of mint.

ELENI'S BAKLAVA

Yields 30–36 servings

Preheat oven to 350 degrees

FILLING

1 lb. shelled walnuts, coarsely ground
1 tbsp. cinnamon
5 tbsp. sugar
Dash cloves
Dash nutmeg (optional)
Grated orange rind (optional)
1 lb. phyllo pastry sheets
1 lb. unsalted butter

Baklava: The queen of Greek pastries

SYRUP

3 cups sugar
3½ cups water
Several whole cloves
Juice of 1 lemon

1. Make syrup:
   - In saucepan combine sugar and cloves in water.
   - Bring to boil and simmer for 20 minutes; add lemon juice after 15 minutes.
   - Remove cloves before cooling.

2. Cool thoroughly, refrigerating to get temperature to cold.
3. Mix walnuts, sugar, and spice together thoroughly. This should make about 4½ cups filling.
4. Melt butter. Brush melted butter on bottom of 13 x 9½ x 2-inch pan.
5. Place 2 phyllo sheets in pan, brushing each sheet with the melted butter as they are laid in it. Sprinkle the top sheet with walnut mixture.*

Continued on next page

(Refrigerate half of the sheets while using up the first half. The sheets that you are using should be kept in a dampened towel.)

6. Repeat step 5 until there are only 6 phyllo sheets left.

7. Spread remaining 6 sheets on the top, one at a time, brushing each sheet with the melted butter as you lay one on top of the other.

8. With a sharp knife cut baklava diagonally into 2-inch diamond-shaped or square pieces. Pour the rest of the melted butter into the cracks between the cut pieces.

9. Bake in oven for 30 minutes, placing pan on middle shelf of oven. Move to top shelf and bake 30 minutes more or until golden brown.

10. Remove from oven and pour the cold syrup over the hot baklava. Cool before serving.

*NOTE

■ To estimate the amount of walnut mixture you need for each layer in step 5, estimate the number of layers you will have and divide that number into approximately 4½ cups of walnut mixture. Example: 24 phyllo sheets in package minus 6 for the top = 18. 18 divided by 2 = 9 layers. 4½ cups (or 9/2) divided by 9 = ½ cup walnut mixture sprinkled on every other sheet.

OPTION

♥ For a more nutritional and traditional tasting syrup use 2 cups sugar and 1 cup honey. Reduce water to 3¼ cups. Boil the lemon peel of the squeezed lemon in the pot while you simmer it. Remove it before cooling.

My Mother's Michigan Kitchen

CHAPTER III

MY MOTHER LEARNS TO COOK

Yaya Eleni, my maternal grandmother, was a master chef. All of her meals were the stuff of legend—perfect in execution, taste, and looks. She cooked vats of food for every holiday and special occasion, even into her old age, when she could barely see and had shrunk to child-size.

But she didn't teach my mother, Angela, to cook. As the master, nobody was allowed to or dared to enter *Yaya*'s kitchen. Besides, Angela, or Angie as she was known, was a social butterfly in her maiden years. She was too busy attending social functions, taking mandolin lessons, or just visiting friends to be in the kitchen. It wasn't until she married my father, Connie (his nickname), that her latent skills were honed to make her the wonderful cook she became.

My parents met at one of the many social functions my mother attended. They were both members of G.A.P.A., short for Greek American Paternal Association, a youth group in which Greeks in their teens and early twenties could go out together. (Couples dating was forbidden at this time, in this culture.) Old photo albums I inherited show this gang of skinny youths picnicking, playing baseball, and standing along the beach in their tight, knitted bathing suits of the

Constantine and Angela Manolakas on their wedding day, June 18, 1939

My mother was clueless in the kitchen when she married my father. Since Connie's major lifetime hobby was eating, her expertise as a cook ranked first and foremost in his mind.

late 1930s. Invariably, in the pictures the girls self-consciously hold their towels up to block our view of their slender figures, while the boys suck in their stomachs and strike muscle man poses.

My parents courted on these outings and on my grandparents' front porch, where Connie feigned visits to Angie's older brother, Gus. They made a handsome couple. My mother had big green eyes, a beautiful smile, an athletic figure, and wavy brown hair. My father had a cute nose and mischievous grin. After a year of courting my father popped the question as they skated arm-in-arm at an outdoor ice-skating party on Belle Isle, a popular recreational park on the Detroit River. Always more practical than romantic, Angela decided to say yes in order to keep her options open. After all, she could always change her mind, she told me, but a negative response could have lost Connie's attentions forever.

Her initial calculation belies their 55 happy years together. My father, ever the romantic, was devoted to her, and she in turn, to him. Always close, after they raised their two children and retired, they were inseparable. They enjoyed doing everything together: singing in the church choir, golfing, going to concerts and plays. My father attended so often, he was even made an honorary member of her church women's club. In her last days, he was at her bedside continuously, willing to do anything to make her feel comfortable and loved. In the beginning, however, there was that one big glitch— Angie couldn't cook.

My parents both told stories about how my mother was clueless in the kitchen when she married my father. Since Connie's major lifetime hobby was eating, her expertise as a cook ranked first and foremost in his mind. I'm not exaggerating, the first and foremost! To meet his ravenous expectations, Angie would phone her mother daily for directions on how to cook those certain dishes on her dinner menu. Her most memorable story of this time was the first time she tried to cook a chicken dinner.

ANGELA'S CHICKEN PILAFI

Serves 4–6 people

Preheat oven to 350 degrees

3–4 lb. whole chicken
1 6-oz. can tomato paste
Garlic granules
Cinnamon
Salt and pepper
1–2 tbsp. butter or margarine
2½ cups boiling water
1 cup raw rice

1. Rinse a whole cleaned chicken; pat it dry. Rub the chicken with 1 tbsp. tomato paste for a thin coating.

2. Sprinkle with garlic granules, cinnamon, salt, and pepper.
3. Dot with butter.
4. Add ½ cup water to the bottom of a roasting pan along with the chicken and bake for 1 hour in a 350-degree oven.
5. Stir the rest of the tomato paste into the remaining 2 cups water, and add it and the rice into the bottom of the pan.
6. Increase the oven temperature to 400 degrees and continue baking for another 30 minutes, basting the chicken occasionally with the tomato sauce until it is absorbed by the rice.

When they got married in 1939 in Detroit, if you wanted to cook a chicken you went to the local butcher and bought a decapitated hen. You then went home, plucked it, burned off the pinfeathers, and cooked the carcass. (Even in the 1950s, when I was a child, I would

ANGELA'S BAKED CHICKEN OREGANI

Serves 4–6 people

Preheat oven to 350 degrees

3–4 lb. whole chicken
Vegetable oil or melted butter or
    margarine
Garlic powder or granules
Salt and pepper
Oregano, preferably Greek
Juice of 1 lemon
Approximately 1 cup water
Potatoes, peeled and quartered
Butter or margarine

Baked Chicken Oregani goes with potatoes
or pilaf

1. Rinse a whole chicken; pat it dry, and
    put it in a roasting pan. Brush it with
    vegetable oil or melted butter (or
    margarine).
2. Sprinkle it with garlic powder, salt, pepper,
    and oregano.
3. Squeeze the juice of 1 lemon over it.
4. Put about 1 cup of water in the bottom
    of the pan and surround the bird with
    peeled and quartered potatoes, which
    have also been sprinkled with salt, pepper,
    garlic powder, oregano and lemon juice.

5. Dot the potatoes with butter or
    margarine.
6. Bake at 350 degrees for about 1½
    hours, or until chicken is tender. Make
    sure you baste the chicken and potatoes
    several times during the baking time
    with the juice at the bottom of the pan.
7. Turn oven up to 400 degrees for the
    last 15–20 minutes to brown both the
    chicken and the potatoes. (Sometime
    the potatoes take longer to cook. If that
    happens remove the chicken and wrap it
    in aluminum foil to keep it warm. Con-
    tinue to cook the potatoes until they
    are soft and browned before serving.)

watch my mother light a candle to burn off the pinfeathers that were still stuck in the skin of the chicken. She would then wash the black candle soot off the bird before putting it into the oven.)

So Angela went to the butcher, bought the bird, and brought it home. But she couldn't pluck it. Instead she sat down and cried for the poor, dead chicken. Then she cried because she knew she couldn't cook the bird for my dad that night, and he would be mightily disappointed. So there my mother sat, in her kitchen hankie still in hand, daubing the tears off her face when Connie came home from work that night.

I never found out what they did that evening. Did he sing her their song, "Come to Me My Melancholy Baby," and then take her out to a restaurant? Did he pluck the chicken for his young wife? And what about the next time she had to cook a chicken? Did she go to a more expensive butcher shop where they de-feathered the bird before sale, thus saving her the heartless task of plucking the chicken herself?

Somehow she overcame her aversion to primitive food preparation and created several excellent chicken recipes. Here are the two that she served most often.

A WORD ABOUT MY FATHER: WHAT'S IN A NAME?

My father's name should have been George Manolakas, since the Greek tradition is to name the first-born son after his paternal grandfather, but he was named Constantine Manolakas instead. The newspaper headline to this event could have read: *Bachelor Godfather Defies Tradition and Names Godson After His Own Father.* The complete story follows.

My family had many surprising name changes. To mention a few, my maiden name isn't really Manolakas; rather it is Yanopappas, the clan name for my father's family, which translates in English to Papajohn. Sometime in the nineteenth century one very large Yannopappa male was named Manolis. Because of this he was called big Manolis or *Manolaka.* He must have been very memorable—either large in stat-

Angela went to the butcher, bought the bird, and brought it home. But she couldn't pluck it. Instead she sat down and cried for the poor, dead chicken.

Connie Manolakas, the newlywed in the kitchen?

ure or large in life—because his nickname became associated with his entire family. The whole lot became referred to as Manolakas.

My mother's maiden name was changed to Carlos when my grandfather came to America and went through the immigrant entry point at Castle Gardens, New York. His original name was Kaloyeropoulos. (Attention opera fans: Maria Callas' name was originally Kaloyeropoulos. There has always been the hopeful claim that our family was related to her.) We all assume that the customs official could neither pronounce nor spell the original name, so he shortened it when he completed my grandfather's paperwork. My cousin Paul, when he was in his thirties, legally changed his name from Carlos back to Kaloyeropoulos, in what must have been a mad pursuit of ethnic purity and tradition. Why else would somebody choose such a long and difficult name? Paul is in the movie industry, and I saw his name once in the credits of a film. It was awesome, spreading across the entire screen.

At the last Manolakas Thanksgiving I attended, I had mentioned these stories to the family. Then my Uncle George Papageorge dropped a bomb: Papageorge wasn't his real last name either. Everybody around the table was surprised, including his son, my cousin Nick, whose jaw dropped as he did a double take. Uncle George explained that his family first settled in West Virginia when they came to America. They lived there until the early 1920s, before my uncle was born, and learned the noble folk art of making moonshine from their neighbors. Not only were they breaking the law on two counts with their illegal profession, since this was during Prohibition, but they also could have been deported. When the Feds came after them the family hightailed it out of the state. They went on the lam, moving north to the Detroit area, and changed their names to Papageorge.

Uncle George's real name is Karahalis, a secret his family had kept from him. He didn't find out about it until he joined the Army in World War II, and his commanding officer called him in one day to

George Papageorge dropped a bomb: Papageorge wasn't his real last name. Everybody around the table was surprised, including his son, my cousin Nick.

ask what my uncle was trying to pull by saying he was a Papageorge. Somehow the C.O. had found records that stated my uncle's name was actually Karahalis. My uncle was dumbfounded. When the officer ordered him to call his father and verify it, the old man confirmed the story and the family's true name. I think they did better with the false moniker of Papageorge and a fresh start.

So I had heard explanations for the changing my family's last names, but I didn't know what caused my father's first name to become Constantine. My mother finally solved the mystery for me when she explained an unusual Greek tradition still practiced when my father was a baby.

At the time of my father's birth, the custom was to not name newborns, but rather wait until their baptisms. In the Greek Church babies might not be baptized for 6 months to more than a year after they are born. Until the baptism, the child was called *Dracos* if it was a boy and *Dracoula* if it was a girl. My initial reaction was to relate the names to Dracula. Thinking I must be wrong, I asked my mother what *dracos* and *dracoula* meant. She pondered, trying to unravel the etymology of the words, and then said, "Pagan." The unbaptized child was not Christian until baptism; therefore, it was a pagan. I was amazed they would call a sweet, innocent child a pagan, because to the Greeks being a pagan is synonymous with being damned, far worse than being called a vampire.

According to custom, on the day of the christening the mother and father would stay at home, and the godparent(s) would take the child to the church. In the narthex (vestibule) of the church the priest would initiate the ceremony with an exorcism and then ask the godparent the child's name. The parents and godparents typically discussed and agreed upon this fine point prior to the occasion, but in actuality, the godparent possessed the freedom to name the child whatever he or she wished. In my father's case, his godfather was a bachelor and would produce no son to receive his father's name. So

His godfather, a bachelor, would produce no son. So at the church he named my father Constantine, to honor his own family.

The sun sank with a blaze of salmon pink, red-orange, and finally purple. Fireflies dotted the nights, serenaded with the subtle sound of waves lapping the shore.

at the door of the church he named my father Constantine, in order to honor his own family.

After the priest announced the baby's name, the children of the community who were present would race to the home of the baby's parents to announce it to them. The child who arrived there first and announced the name was given money or a gift in return. I can imagine the fast pace of that race to my grandparents' home, with the children motivated by the purse that awaited the winner. I can further imagine my grandparents' surprise and consternation upon learning that their first-born son's name was not George, after his grandfather, but Constantine.

My father didn't mind. In fact, he liked his name, especially his nicknames of Connie and Coke (because he tanned as dark as coke in the summer), and he loved his godfather. After all, it was his godfather who owned the ice cream parlor where my father worked as a soda jerk in his youth. During his employment he was allowed to eat a pint of ice cream a day, and he took full advantage of that perk. To my dad, free ice cream was more important than any name.

SUMMERTIME BARBECUE

For the first ten years of my life, my family lived in Detroit, Michigan, from September to June. We spent our summers, however, in a small cottage on beautiful Lake St. Clair in Ontario, Canada. At the cottage we were surrounded by the wonders of nature, including many hot summer twilights, when the sun sank into this little lake with a blaze of colors: salmon pink, red-orange, and finally purple. Fireflies dotted the nights, which were serenaded with the subtle sound of waves steadily lapping on the shore. Each summer was also memorable for its abundant, fresh food and my parents' constant entertaining.

My father, Connie, built the two-bedroom cottage by himself before I was born. Since it was just across the U.S.-Canadian border, we only drove an hour to reach it from our home in Detroit. My father's work in downtown Detroit was a half hour away from both houses. It was basic in design, with a white clapboard exterior, red-shingled roof, and green linoleum floors throughout. The screened-in back porch overlooking the lake and the large living room picture window with its view of the front yard were it's best features. The only source of heat my father provided during damp, cold weather was the fireplace in the living room, and he never finished the ceilings in the shower and the closets, providing easy access to the many spiders that shared the house with us. But the cottage was a snug and homey place in the summer and the site for 10 years of good times.

Our home stood between the cottage of his best friend of many years, Pete Stevens, and the one owned by Yaya Despina, Aunt Ginny, and Uncle George Papageorge. My father also built a brick barbecue, a classic design with a square brick chimney and two side shelves of formed cement. It stood with its back to the lake in a yard that also boasted a picnic table and benches that seated twelve.

In nature's stunning sunset light show we feasted on freshly picked barbecued corn with our dinners. On the weekends, the barbecue started late in the afternoon and went on into the evening—my father cooking barbecued chicken or lamb *shish-kebab* (also called *souvlakia*), as well as the ever-popular hamburgers and hot dogs. The children played on the shore, breathing in the tantalizing aromas of the meats as they sizzled on the fire. With both Independence Day and my brother Stan's birthday, July was party month at our place. Throngs of family and friends joined us for water sports, card games, and the Greek national sport—eating.

The picnic table groaned under the weight of so many Greek and American dishes—from *souvlakia*, Greek salad, braised okra or green beans to Jell-O molds and potato salad. For dessert we feasted on cold, crunchy watermelon, iced in a round aluminum wash tub, and *baklava*, peach cobbler, various *koulourakia*, berry pies, and citrus spoon sweets.

Connie's Arni Souvlakia—Shish Kebab

Yields 6–8 servings

Leg of lamb
1 cup olive oil
1/3 cup lemon juice
1/2 cup wine
Salt and pepper
2 cloves garlic, minced
1–2 bay leaves
Tomatoes—quartered
Onions—quartered and separated
Green Pepper—cut in 1 1/2 inch squares
Mushroom caps

Skewer your marinated meat and vegetables before cooking.

1. Cut lamb off the bone and into 1–2 inch cubes.
2. Mix marinade of olive oil, lemon juice, wine, garlic, and spices.
3. Put lamb chunks and vegetables in a deep, large pot. Pour in marinade, and gently toss the mixture in the marinade.
4. Weigh down the mixture with a plate pressed on top, and refrigerate for 2–3 hours, tossing occasionally.
5. Put meat and vegetables alternately on skewers (8–12 skewers depending on their length).
6. Barbecue or broil about 15–20 minutes, turning occasionally, until the meat is cooked and yet the vegetables are still intact.

Options

- Use 2 pounds beefsteak or buffalo steaks, cut into 1–2 inch cubes instead of the lamb.
- Use cherry tomatoes, instead of quartered tomatoes. They stay intact on the skewer.

Connie's Greek Barbecued Chicken

Yields 4 servings

2½–3 lb. broiler or fryer, cut into
    serving pieces
Garlic granules
Salt and pepper to taste
1½ tsp. oregano
Juice of 1 lemon
¼ cup white wine or water
⅓ cup melted butter

Grandson Asher Hawes chows down on a
barbecued chicken leg

1. Several hours ahead or the day before,
   place chicken in a deep bowl or pot.
2. Mix wine (or water) and lemon juice;
   pour over chicken pieces. Sprinkle each
   piece liberally with garlic granules, then
   with the salt, pepper, and oregano.
3. Cover the bowl and refrigerate.
4. About 45 minutes before cooking, brush
   the chicken with melted butter and place
   it on a plate separate from the marinade.
   Refrigerate the chicken until it is time to
   cook it. Pour the remaining butter into
   the marinade left in the bowl, and reserve
   the mixture for basting.
5. Barbecue the chicken on a medium fire,
   or broil it in the oven, 3 to 4 inches
   from the heat source. Cook 20 minutes
   on each side, basting often with the
   marinade. Make sure that the chicken is
   cooked thoroughly to the bone.

Option

To hasten cooking time, microwave the
chicken pieces on high for 10 minutes. Barbecue or broil the pieces for about 20–30
minutes, basting and turning them frequently.

CONNIE'S BROILED OR BARBECUED FISH

Serves 4

1 ½–2 lbs. firm, white fish (such as
    mackerel or bass) cut in serving
    size pieces
½ cup olive oil
Juice of 2 lemons
2–3 cloves garlic, minced
Dried or fresh oregano
Salt and pepper
Parsley and lemon slices

1. Make a marinade of the olive oil, lemon, and garlic.
2. Rinse the fish in water; pat dry; and immerse it in marinade.
3. Refrigerate for 1 hour.
4. Take the fish from the marinade, and sprinkle both sides with salt, pepper, and oregano.
5. Broil or barbecue the fish on one side for 10 minutes.
6. Brush the uncooked side with marinade , then turn the fish over, the uncooked side to flame. Barbecue 10 more minutes.
7. Serve garnished with parsley and lemon slices.

On Independence Day we followed our feast with a colorful display of fireworks, such as pinwheels and roman candles, we shot off over the lake into the star-spangled sky. We children were thrilled when the adults lit strings of popping firecrackers or we wrote our names in the evening air with sparklers and watched black ash snakes grow from the Smokey Joes. The next day the young woke up early to dig out the smoky-smelling remnants of the fireworks from the sand—reliving, with tales and lively descriptions, the marvels of the fiery night.

MORE SUMMER COOKING

Our cottage was surrounded by farmland, which provided a steady supply of fresh fruits and vegetables for my mother's kitchen. While my brother and I swam, fished, and played outdoors on sunny days, or played Monopoly, Parcheesi, Sorry, and Clue when it rained, my mother prepared a steady stream of delectable meals, desserts, and canned and preserved fruits and vegetables.

We would pick our own strawberries out of local farmers' fields, which would end up in pies and in wax-topped jars of strawberry preserves. My father, who continued to work throughout the summer as a draftsman, would purchase freshly picked corn on his way home from the office. The ears from the Green Giant growing fields cost two for a penny or ten cents a dozen. My father roasted those ears on the barbecue. My mother canned peaches, made peach preserves, and concocted a marvelous chili sauce, all of which carried the luscious taste of summer into the cold months of our Detroit winters. She made her pies and cobblers from scratch. I especially loved her blueberry pies and peach cobblers.

Because my parents entertained every weekend, cooking for their many friends and family who were escaping the heat and humidity of the city, my mother made

The young woke up early to dig out the smoky-smelling remnants of the fireworks from the sand, reliving the marvels of the fiery night.

Stanton's eighth birthday party, at our cottage in Belle River, Ontario, Canada

ANGELA'S PASTITSIO

Yields 16 servings

Preheat oven 400 degrees

MEAT SAUCE

4 tbsp. butter

3 onions, chopped

3 cloves garlic, minced

1–1½ lbs. ground meat

1 28-oz. can of whole tomatoes,
    coarsely chopped

1 8-oz. tomato sauce (optional)

1 cinnamon stick

2 tsp. oregano

Salt and pepper to taste

½ cup bread crumbs

1¼ lb. macaroni (see notes)

Grated Romano or parmesan cheese

CUSTARD SAUCE

¾ cup butter

½ cup flour

1½ qt. milk, heated to simmering

9 eggs

Pastitsio: A hint of cinnamon and a creamy sauce makes this casserole divine

1. Brown onions, garlic, and meat in melted butter.
2. Add tomatoes, spices, and seasonings. Cover and simmer for 1 hour.
3. Cool and stir in half of the breadcrumbs.
4. Cook macaroni according to the directions of the package. Drain, but do not rinse.

Continued on next page

5. Make the custard sauce: Brown the flour lightly in melted butter. Add hot milk to the browned flour, stirring constantly. Cook over low heat until the sauce is thick. Beat the 9 eggs well, and add the hot milk and flour mixture to the eggs very slowly, so they don't curdle.

6. Sprinkle remaining breadcrumbs into a buttered 11 x 16 x 2 inch-baking pan. Put in a layer of half the macaroni, a layer of half the meat sauce, and pour about one third of the custard sauce over the top of that layer. Sprinkle with grated cheese.

7. Put in another layer of macaroni and meat, and sprinkle with cheese. Pour about half the remaining custard sauce on top, and bake in a 400-degree oven for five minutes.

8. Remove from oven, and pour the remaining custard sauce on top of the casserole. Sprinkle with grated cheese.

9. Reduce oven temperature to 325 degrees, and bake for 40 to 50 minutes or until custard is set and lightly browned.

NOTES

- ♥ Ground meat can be beef, or turkey or buffalo for leaner options
- ■ Either ziti or elbow macaroni can be used. I prefer ziti.

vats of potato salad, Greek salad, and fresh vegetables—*fassoulakia* (green beans in tomato sauce), *bamias* (okra stewed in tomato sauce), and spinach with olive oil and lemon. My Yaya Eleni and Aunt Kathryn would bring the *pastitsio* (Greek-style lasagna) or *tiropites* and *spanakopita* (cheese and spinach pies made of thin, crisp phyllo dough).

One dish Mom made typifies to me the taste of those summer feasts. Because they were in abundant supply during the summer months, my mother would stuff fresh tomatoes and green peppers with a savory meat and rice filling, and then bake them until they

ANGELA'S STUFFED TOMATOES AND GREEN PEPPERS

Yields 4–6 servings

Preheat oven to 350 degrees

5 tbsp. butter
2 yellow onions, chopped
1½ lbs. ground meat
Salt and pepper
⅓ cup chopped fresh parsley
2 tbsp. finely chopped fresh mint
½ cup raw white rice
Tomatoes
Green peppers
1 cup water

Stuff your summer produce with a savory meat and rice mixture

1. The number of tomatoes and peppers used will vary because of their sizes and your preference for tomatoes versus peppers. Estimate 8–10 for the total number of vegetables. Cut thin slices off the tops of the vegetables; save. Scoop out the insides to leave empty shells, saving the insides of each vegetable, except the green pepper seeds. Chop up the saved insides (including the white fiber inside the pepper).

2. Melt 3 tbsp. butter in a large frying pan. Sauté the onions until tender and translucent.

3. Add the ground meat and brown thoroughly.

4. Add the seasonings and spices, and stir until the fresh spices are wilted. Mix in raw rice.

5. Stir the chopped insides of the vegetables (reserved from step 1) into the meat mixture. Simmer on low heat for about 5 minutes.

Continued on next page

6. Sprinkle the insides of the tomatoes and green peppers with salt, and fill them to the tops with the meat and rice mixture, leaving only enough room for their caps. Place in a baking dish, and dot the tops of the vegetables with butter; then place the caps of the vegetables on top to cover the meat mixture. (Any extra filling can be placed in the bottom of the casserole dish.)

7. Pour a cup of water in the bottom of the pan, and bake in the preheated oven for 1 hour or until the vegetables and rice are cooked. Baste the vegetables occasionally with the liquid from the bottom of the baking dish.

OPTIONS

- ♥ Use olive oil instead of butter for a dish with less saturated fat.
- ♥ Substitute brown basmati rice (available in bulk at gourmet or health-food stores) for white rice. It has the same texture and taste as white rice, but has the added nutrients of an unrefined grain. Precook it 20 minutes in 1 cup of water before adding it to the ground meat mixture. There should be very little water left in the pan after the precooking, which can be added to the mixture as well.
- ■ Ground meat can be the traditional mix of beef and lamb, or you may try all lamb or ground beef, or ground buffalo or turkey for leaner options.
- ■ This is traditionally a seasonal summer dish when fresh tomatoes, green peppers, parsley and mint are in good supply. If you are cooking this dish off-season and are using dried spices, substitute 1 tbsp. dried parsley and 1 tsp. dried mint for the fresh ingredients.
- ■ For a richer sauce mix 3 tbsp. tomato paste with the water added to the bottom of the pan.

were soft, succulent, and tasting of the fresh mint she grew in the flowerbeds around the cottage. She served them with fresh barbecued corn, Greek bread and salad, feta cheese and olives—an excellent summer meal. When I make and taste them today, I am transported back to the summers of my youth, reminded of the good times, dear friends and family, and the hearty meals of those sultry bygone days.

ELENI'S TIROPITES—GREEK CHEESE PUFFS

Yields 72–90

Preheat oven 375 degrees

½ lb. feta cheese, chopped in small
    chunks
½ lb. carton cottage cheese
3 eggs, well beaten
½ cup fresh parsley or dill, chopped
    fine
1 to 1–½ lb. phyllo dough
1 ¼–½ cup butter

1. Mix together the cheeses, eggs, and spices.
2. Let mixture stand overnight, in refrigerator.
3. Preheat oven to 375–400 degrees (depending on your oven).
4. Melt the butter.
5. Cut the phyllo dough into 4 4-inch strips. Refrigerate all but the stack of strips you are using, which should be kept in a dampened towel.
6. For each tiropita, remove 1 strip of phyllo and lay it on a smooth clean surface. Brush with melted butter. Fold in half,

Tiropites: folded triangles of crispy phyllo stuffed with a savory cheese filling

Continued on next page

lengthwise to produce a double-layered 2-inch strip. Brush again with butter. Place 1 rounded tsp. of the cheese and egg mixture in the upper right-hand corner of the phyllo strip. Fold right corner over the mixture to form a triangle at the top of the strip; then fold the triangle carefully down the strip, keeping the mixture snug in the triangle and preserving the shape. Continue to fold the triangle over to the right and down, over to the left and down, until the whole strip has been wrapped around the triangle. Lightly butter finished triangle and press end flap of the strip to buttered triangle to form a light seal.

7. Place each triangle on a cookie sheet about 1 inch apart.

8. Bake approximately 20 minutes, until golden brown and crispy.

9. Allow them to cool about 10 minutes. (The inside cheese mixture will be molten when removed from oven.) Serve warm.

NOTES

- If using fresh parsley, you may also want to add ½ tsp. dried dill.
- The tiropites can be frozen unbaked (freeze in separated layers) and baked before serving for 25–30 minutes, until crispy and golden.

ANGELA'S PEACH COBBLER

Yields 10–12 servings

Preheat oven 400 degrees

FILLING

1 cup sugar
1½ tbsp. cornstarch
¼ tsp. salt
½ cup water
7–8 cups fresh free-stone peaches, sliced
1 tbsp. lemon juice
1¼ tsp. almond extract
½ tbsp. lemon peel

CRUST

3⅔ cups baking mix (e.g. Bisquick)
1 cup milk
4½ tbsp. sugar
5 tbsp. butter, melted

1. In a saucepan, mix the sugar, cornstarch, salt, and water.
2. Bring to boil and boil 1 minute. Then let the mixture cool to lukewarm.
3. Add sliced peaches to the boiled, cooled mixture. Mix together the lemon juice, almond extract, and lemon peel. Stir this mixture into the peach mixture.
4. Arrange peach mixture in greased 9½-inch x 13-inch pan.
5. Prepare the shortcake by mixing together the baking mix, milk, sugar, and melted butter.
6. Spoon the shortcake over top of the peaches, spreading to the edges of the pan. Lightly sprinkle sugar on the top.
7. Bake 30–40 minutes, until the crust is lightly browned.

OPTIONS

- ♥ A later notation on my mother's recipe suggests using 5 tsp. artificial sweetener instead of sugar. This suggestion might be useful for diabetics.
- ■ Another of her later notations suggests microwaving the fruit mixture for 7 minutes, stirring several times. I have never done it that way and believe that if you get ripe peaches this step is unnecessary and may destroy the nutrients in the peaches.

ANGELA'S FASSOLAKIA—BRAISED GREEN BEANS

Yields 6–8 servings

1 large onion, chopped
2–3 cloves garlic, minced
2 tbsp. olive oil (+1 tbsp., optional)
1 6-oz. can of tomato paste
1½–2 cups water
2–3 lbs. fresh string beans
Fresh parsley and/or mint, chopped
¼ tsp. salt
⅛ tsp. pepper
1 tsp. dried oregano
Dash dill

Herbed green beans in tomato sauce complements meat and poultry dishes

1. Rinse the beans; cut off their tips; and cut the beans in 2–3 inch lengths.
2. Sauté the onion and garlic in 2 tbsp. olive oil until soft and translucent.
3. Add the tomato paste and water, and stir until the tomato paste is well mixed.
4. Add the string beans and seasonings. Cover and cook until the beans are tender, 20–30 minutes.
5. In the last several minutes you can add 1 more tbsp. of olive oil for a richer tasting dish.

NOTE

If you use frozen string beans, 2 pounds will be sufficient.

THE STRAW, THE BEAN, AND THE COAL

When I was growing up, all of my family members belonged to the Greek Orthodox Church, which requires fasts of its faithful during Lent, as well as Wednesdays and Fridays. It encourages the strictest of fasts: omitting olive oil, alcohol, all animal products, and fish, while for some reason allowing invertebrates, i.e., shrimp, mussels, squid. In America, the faithful mostly fast from meat.

When I grew up my family honored the no meat on Friday practice throughout the year. We also abstained from all meat, dairy, eggs, and fish on Wednesdays and Fridays when we prepared for Communion and during Lent. For us children, the hardest part of the Communion fast was to eat no food or drink, even water, between dinner on Friday night until after we received the Host at the special children's service the following Saturday morning. By the time we had sat through the long morning service, with its high ritual and Greek hymns, I thought everybody in the pews around me could hear my stomach growling. Then we waited in long lines to receive Communion—a tiny spoonful of wine and a small scrap of bread from the priest's chalice. At the end this near-starvation, the Sunday School students received a small cube of "holy bread" and marched down to the church's large basement where the ladies of the church fed us orange juice, small boxes of Kellogg's Frosted Flakes with milk, and glazed doughnuts or sweet rolls. After near-death, we became euphoric on our spiritual blessings and sugar highs.

During our fasts my mother served her family beans, lentils, rice, and vegetables. The three dishes I remember are black-eyed beans and rice (*fassolorizo*), spinach and rice (*spanikorizo*), and lentil soup. I loved the first two meals, but to my uneducated palate the soup tasted like sin and repentance.

My affection for black-eyed beans was based not only on its creamy tomato taste, but also the expectation that whenever she served this

After near-death, we became euphoric on our spiritual blessings and sugar highs.

dish my mother would tell my brother Stanton and me the story of "How the Black-Eyed Bean Got Its Mark." I loved the story, and even when I was ten, well past the need for a nursery tale, I demanded she retell it every time. Here is the story she told:

> One day three good friends—the Straw, the Bean, and the Coal—were walking in the country having a good time. Coal carried a kerchief full of provisions and useful odds and ends, suspended on the end of a stick slung over his shoulder. They walked along until they came to a rocky stream that obstructed their path. They stood there, looking at the obstacle, wondering how they could cross the stream and be on their way.
>
> Straw had an idea, "I'll fall across the stream to form a bridge over which the two of you can cross. Then you can haul me up from the other side, and we can be on our way."
>
> The three heatedly discussed the idea. Coal was all for it, but Bean exclaimed, "No! I won't do it. Have you forgotten I'm afraid of heights? I'll fall off Straw for sure and hit the rocks and stream below." However, with no other means in sight and reassurance from his friends, Bean finally agreed to follow Straw's plan.
>
> Straw flopped himself over the creek ravine and invited his friends to cross, assuring them that he was strong enough to hold their weight. Coal went first to show his friend, Bean, that it was safe and could indeed be done. Bean was still timid and had to be cajoled by his friends, but finally, after much coaxing, Bean started to walk carefully across.
>
> Coal called to him, "Don't look down, Bean. Keep your eyes on me instead."
>
> Bean did this until just past the midpoint of the ravine, when a bird flew out of the surrounding wood and distracted him from his view of Coal at the far side of the creek. He looked down without thinking and became frightened at what he saw. His

perch was far above the rocks and swift-flowing water. Distracted by his fear, he lost his balance, and with a squawk, he fell off the straw onto the rocks below. When he hit the rocks he split open, right down the middle of his front seam. His friends stood there shocked into stillness, aghast at his fall.

Bean cried out to them, "Help me! Help! I've fallen down and split open, and I can't get up!"

Coal was startled into action and quickly drew Straw back from across the stream, laying him from the edge of the far bank down to the stream below. He scurried down Straw's back, out to the rocks where Bean lay. Pulling his friend to shore, he reached into his bundle and took out a needle and thread. The only thread he had was black, but he used it anyway. As he worked, carefully sewing up Bean's split seam, the thread made a small circle of black around the closing incision. The small white bean now had a "black eye" where the split had been sewn.

Coal apologized to his friend for the black eye, but Bean said, "Are you kidding? You saved my life. This black eye will remind me of that forever." They climbed up Straw to the bank on the other side of the stream, drew him up, and continued, arm in arm, on their way.

And that is how the black-eyed bean got his black eye!

By the time my mother had finished the story, my brother and I had eaten our bowls of black-eyed beans and rice. And I learned about the value of loyal and helpful friends. The recipe for this Lenten dish is on page 66 and one other follows.

ANGELA'S FASSOLOURIZO—BLACK EYED BEANS AND RICE

Serves 6–8

8 oz. dried black-eyed beans
1 medium onion chopped
2 cloves garlic, minced
2 Tbsp. olive oil
¾ cup brown or white rice
4 cups water
8-oz. can tomato sauce
3-oz. can tomato paste
2 tsp. salt
¼ tsp. pepper
2 tsp. dill
1 bay leaf
Lemon juice to taste

Black-eyed beans in a creamy dill tomato sauce

1. To prepare the beans for cooking, wash them in cold water and drain. Place beans in a 2 qt. pan, cover with cold water, discarding the floaters. Soak the beans for 8 hours in a cool place. Drain.
2. Sauté the onions and garlic in oil in a clean 2 qt. pot until tender and translucent.
3. Add the beans, rice, and water to the pot.
4. Stir in the tomato sauce and paste and the spices.
5. Bring the mixture to a boil and then cover and simmer, stirring occasionally. Simmer 1½-2 hours or until the beans are tender and the mixture is a thick stew.

OPTIONS

♥ My mother used white rice. I prefer brown rice (brown basmati is the best) because of its better nutritional value.

ANGELA'S FAHKI—LENTEN LENTIL SOUP

1 lb. lentils
2 quarts + 2 cups water
½ cup olive oil
1 cup chopped celery
½–¾ cup chopped onions
½ cup chopped carrots
1 cup chopped fresh parsley
1 Tbsp. tomato paste
2 cloves garlic, minced
1 bay leaf
3–4 tsp. salt
⅛–¼ tsp. pepper
½ tsp. dried oregano
3 Tbsp. vinegar
½ Tbsp. flour

1. Rinse lentils and cover with 2 quarts of water.
2. Bring to boil and let simmer 35–40 minutes, until tender.
3. Sauté celery, onions, carrots, and parsley in olive oil until celery is soft and translucent.
4. Add the vegetables, spices and tomato paste, and approximately 2 cups more water. Simmer the soup for 35–40 minutes, until the vegetables are tender.
5. Mix flour and vinegar into a paste. Just before serving, add to the soup and cook a few minutes longer to slightly thicken it.

KITCHEN CAPERS

About the same time the Straw, Bean, and Coal story was popular, Stan and I spent a lot of time with our two cousins, Sandy and Brian Backos, my Aunt Kathryn and Uncle Don's sons. Aunt Kathryn was my mother's younger sister, and the two of them were very close, especially when they were rearing their children, who were all within four years of each

Stan, Sandy, and I were the gang, and Brian was the target.

other in age. We kids spent a lot of time getting in trouble together, so many of our family home movies captured episodes of playful disobedience. One reel catches us in the basement of my Aunt and Uncle's house, Sandy playing the drums and Stanton pounding on the piano. Even in the silent movie, one can tell that volume took precedence over tune. I'm dancing wildly as Brian stands in the midst of us blinking and grimacing at the bright bar of lights across my father's 8-mm movie camera. The adults line the stairs down into the basement holding their hands to their ears, except for my aunt and my mother. They are visibly yelling at us and gesturing to keep the noise down.

As sometimes happens, the three older children ganged up on the youngest. Stan, Sandy, and I were the gang, and Brian was the target. It didn't help Brian's cause that as a child he suffered from some physical frailties, which fully unloosed my aunt's protective motherly instincts. It was not Brian's frailties that incited us as much as the special treatment we thought he received because of them. We tried to balance this out with special treatment of our own.

I have one vivid memory of my aunt's care for Brian when I was eight. Brian was about six years old, and our gang had made a makeshift teeter-totter by putting a long wooden plank over a low breakwater wall at our lakeside cottage. Of course, Brian had to fall off of it. As his end of the board flew up, he flew off and landed with a loud thud on the grass. He lay there in shock for a few seconds, the wind knocked out of him. All the other children stopped their running and yelling and stood silently looking at him, as if we were all holding our collective breath, thinking he might be hurt or we might get into big trouble. My concern turned into cold-hearted disdain when he gathered his wind and his wits and I heard him cry for his Mommy.

She jumped up, gathered her full skirt and crinoline petticoat, and ran in her platform mules across the yard. I stood in awe as she cleared a three-foot hedge.

Aunt Kathryn was and still is the glamorous, lady-like type. She dresses in Vogue Magazine fashions and was the first woman in the family to color her hair—a rich, brassy red. She has always looked stunning. I noticed Aunt Kathryn 100 feet away in the next yard,

ANGELA'S SPANAKORIZO—SPINACH AND RICE

Serves 4

1 medium onion, chopped
1 tbsp. olive oil
1 bunch fresh spinach or 1 pkg. frozen
    chopped spinach
½ cup rice
¾ cup water
8-oz. can tomato sauce
¼ cup chopped fresh parsley
½ tsp. dried dill
Salt and pepper to taste

1. Brown onion in olive oil until soft.
2. Add spinach and rice.
3. Pour in water, tomato sauce, and seasonings. Stir and bring to boil.
4. Cover and steam rice about 30 minutes or until done, stirring occasionally.

OPTION

To double the recipe, use a 15-oz. can of tomato sauce; the rest of the ingredients are doubled.

gossiping with a circle of women, when she heard Brian's cry. She immediately jumped up, gathered her full skirt and crinoline petticoat high up on her hips, and ran in her platform mules across the yard. I stood in awe as she leapt over a three-foot hedge. I mean she cleared it! As she jumped she screamed, "Briiiii—an," in her high soprano voice. Without pause she rushed to his side. Of course, Brian wasn't really hurt, and of course, the gang grumbled when Brian was pulled onto my aunt's lap. Then all the ladies in the circle cooed over him and, to sooth his ruffled sensibilities, found him something especially delicious to eat, most likely my yaya's *koulourakia*.

Brian grabbed the plastic mustard bottle and squeezed with all his might. A great glob of yellow mustard shot out, flew high in the air, and splatted on the white ceiling of the kitchen.

Our hazing continued both summer and winter until we all finally grew up. One trick we particularly liked to play on Brian happened when we gathered for dinners at my Aunt and Uncle's house. While the adults occupied the dining room, the children were relegated, as usual, to the kitchen. Aunt Kathryn's kitchen was tiny, just large enough for a kitchen table the size of a card-table. Though it was situated only eight feet from where our parents sat, we were hidden from their view by the kitchen wall. Invisibility allowed us the freedom to bedevil Brian without our parents noticing.

The trick went like this: Somebody would yell, "Whoever likes peanut butter (or chocolate or Greek cheese), touch the salt shaker." And then all of us kids would rush to touch the shaker. Whoever touched it first could claim to like it best.

"Whoever likes cherry popsicles (or ice cream or *baklava*) raise your fork in the air." Four forks would be raised.

"Whoever likes okra (or squid or Brussels sprouts) pick up your glass of milk." Nobody would move on that one but Brian—not because he liked okra (or squid or Brussels sprouts), but because in his excitement he automatically followed the direction. We would then taunt him for claiming to like the distasteful offering. The simple game would go on a few more rounds, our recklessness growing. Then it was time for the trick.

My brother Stan would pick something that we knew Brian was crazy for, and he would call it out. One time he shouted, "Whoever likes corn on the cob, squeeze the mustard bottle." The three of us instinctively knew to sit back as Brian quickly grabbed the plastic mustard bottle and squeezed with all his might. We watched in wonder as a great glob of yellow mustard shot out of the bottle, flew high up in the air, and splatted on the white ceiling of the kitchen.

We three screamed with laughter, and then loudly proclaimed the damning words, "Brian, look what you did!" We sat innocently, like little angels, as Brian got into trouble, and Uncle Don climbed up on a chair to wipe the mustard from the ceiling. We got him another time with, "If you like orange pop, squeeze the butter." Since my aunt always left her butter at room temperature, as he grabbed and squeezed the cube, the soft fat oozed out through his fingers and coated his hands. We all took heat on that one; by then our parents had figured out our game.

Fortunately, the effects of our teasing bounced off the boy. He grew up to be a successful and compassionate man, an automotive engineer and a wonderful and caring husband and father. I would like to think the rest of the gang of four grew up to be as nice and compassionate as he did.

Angela's *spanakorizo* is another Lenten recipe from those years. If anyone had yelled out, "Whoever likes *spanakorizo* raise your fork in the air," all four of our forks would be raised up high.

Home for the Holidays

CHAPTER IV

THANKSGIVING

I don't understand why the plots of modern movies usually show how people hate to go home to their families during the holidays. Or how when they get there, their visit is a horror show filled with dread, simmering resentments, and outright screaming arguments. My family holidays were happy occasions, with jokes and games and treasured traditions. Based on my own experience, I would never want to go anywhere else. Who else would you want to be with for those special days except your family members—people who know you, are so happy to see you, and love you in their own unique way? When I was growing up, my family's own unique way was with lots of food and lots of loud talk and laughter.

We lived in Detroit until I was almost eleven. Most of our extended family lived there, and we did double duty on each holiday. We visited both my mother's and my father's families, or we combined them all at our house. The combo really worked well on Thanksgiving, when each year we waited for Uncle George Papageorge to return from the annual Detroit Lions' football game before starting our sumptuous dinner of turkey, Greek stuffing, candied sweet potatoes, roast potatoes, Waldorf salad, cauliflower with cheese sauce, Greek and American pumpkin

Who else would you want to be with for those special days except your family members— people who love you in their own unique way?

ANGELA'S CANDIED YAMS

Yields 12–15 servings

Preheat oven to 400 degrees

4 lbs. yams
½ cup butter or margarine
½ cup water
⅓ cup brown sugar
2 oranges, halved and sliced into ¼ inch
    slices
1 cup orange juice

1. Parboil the yams in their jackets, i.e., cook partially by boiling about 25 minutes. Yams should still be firm.
2. Peel and slice into ¾ inch slices; arrange in a large roasting pan.
3. To make syrup: melt together butter, water, brown sugar, and orange juice; add orange slices. Simmer for 25 minutes, until liquid is syrupy.
4. Pour the syrup over the yam slices; arrange the orange slices on top.
5. Bake about 1–1½ hours, basting the yams with the syrup every 15 minutes, until they and the orange slices have a shiny glaze and are slightly browned.

OPTIONS

- ♥ Substitute ⅓ cup maple syrup or ⅓ cup honey for the sugar.
- ■ Add ½ tsp. cinnamon to the syrup.
- ■ Substitute 1 can crushed pineapple for the oranges. Reserve pineapple liquid and add orange juice to make 1 cup of juice.
- ■ Sprinkle the tops of the yams with chopped pecans before baking.

pies, and mince pies. The adults sat in the formal dining room, while the children were left to kid around in the kitchen.

Each Thanksgiving morning, while my dad, brother, and I went to the J. L. Hudson's Thanksgiving Day Parade along Woodward

ANGELA'S CRANBERRY SAUCE

1 12-oz. bag of fresh cranberries
1½ cups sugar
¾ cup water
¾ cup apples, peeled and cut in small pieces
8-oz. can unsweetened crushed pineapple, drained
Dash cinnamon, nutmeg, and cloves
Grated peel of 1 lemon
1 tbsp. grated orange peel

1. Bring the water and sugar to a boil.
2. Add the washed cranberries, apple, pineapple, and grated citrus peels.
3. Add the spices and cook about 15 minutes or until cranberries start to pop.

OPTIONS

♥ Use healthier sweeteners by substituting the pineapple juice from the canned pineapple and apple or orange juice for the water and ½ cup honey or agave syrup instead of the sugar. Using this option produces a tangier, more refreshing sauce.
■ My mother sometimes also added chopped pecans to the sauce—very good.
■ I have made this recipe using fresh pineapple or substituting ½ cup apple pieces and ⅓ cup orange pieces for ¾ cup apple pieces—also very good.

Avenue in downtown Detroit, my mother stayed home in peaceful solitude to start the meal preparations. The last year we went to the parade was in 1957, on a frigid day when the snow swirled down while the majorettes marched by in their short skirts and bare legs. We wondered how they could stand the cold. We shivered as we watched the bands, floats, and equestrians pass by, even though we were dressed in our warm coats, gloves, hats, and woolen scarves. However, we were

ELENI'S TURKEY GRAVY

3 tbsp. reserved pan drippings
2 cups water, turkey, or chicken broth
Giblets, cooked and chopped (optional)
3 tbsp. flour
Salt and pepper to taste

1. Reserve 3 tbsp. turkey drippings from roasting pan, pouring off remaining fat.
2. Pour the water or broth into the roasting pan, scraping to add the browned turkey bits to the liquid.
3. Heat drippings in saucepan and whisk in flour, 1 tbsp. at a time to minimize lumps.
4. Add the pan liquid to the drippings and flour mixture and bring to boil, stirring constantly. Simmer for about 5 minutes, or until it is slightly thickened.
5. Season to taste with salt and pepper.
6. Cooked and chopped giblets, liver, and kidney may be added to the finished gravy and warmed through before serving.

not going to leave before Santa Claus drove by, on the last float of the parade. Old Santy sat on top of a large sleigh complete with his nine reindeer, Rudolph leading the way with his blinking red nose. The jolly old man laughed and waved to everybody in the crowd as he passed, and Stan and I wildly waved back at him, excited to see him, despite the fact that we had outgrown our belief in him. After the festive climax, Pa drove us back to our warm home in his 1956 Chevy Bel Air, to be greeted at the door by the wonderful aromas from my mother's holiday cooking.

When we moved to California, we had only part of the loud, energetic Manolakas family with whom to feast. At first there were only my family and the family of my father's brother, Dr. George Manolakas. Uncle Lee's family, who also lived close by, dined with his in-laws, the Kirlakitsis's, most Thanksgivings. Even at that, the table was full. There were four parents, seven children, and at least four friends to sit down at the holiday table. In the early 1960s *Yaya* Despina and Aunt Ginny and her family moved to California and added four more to our party.

Thanksgiving 1961: Yaya Despina with her sons and their families at Angie and Connie's house.

Several events happened that we could count on gracing the day. My Uncle George Manolakas, a surgeon, would carve the turkey carcass as carefully as if it were a patient of his and then typically be called away for emergency surgery in the middle of the meal. When the party was at Aunt Betty and Uncle George's house, their neighbor Richard, who was my cousin George's friend, would be at the table. (I always wondered why his mother never called him home.) My cousin Sam, slightly younger than my brother and easily the most godless among us, would lead us children in the yearly Thanksgiving cheer: "2-4-6-8 who do we appreciate? Yay, God!" And my cousin Dale and I would square off for our yearly contests.

The Manolakas' are a proud lot and very competitive. Dale and I, two young girls six weeks apart in age, were no exception. During our high-school years we competed for grades and boyfriends. And every Thanksgiving we faced off as well. First we had eating contests, where we tried to outdo each other with the number and size of our servings. Then we staged the water-drinking contests, which probably saved our lives by washing all that stuffing out of our systems. At that point, when we were so uncomfortable we could barely move, we mounted our athletic competitions—seeing who could run the fastest in a series of races or throw a ball the longest distance. When we approached sixteen years old we came to our senses and called a truce, choosing spirited debate as our holiday competition of choice.

My cousin Sam, easily the most godless among us, would lead us children in the yearly Thanksgiving cheer: "2-4-6-8 who do we appreciate? Yay, God!"

ELENI'S GREEK STUFFING

1 lb. round steak, ground
2 tbsp. olive oil
2 tbsp. butter
1 bunch green onions, chopped
3 tbsp. fresh parsley, chopped
1 tbsp. fresh mint, chopped
1 clove garlic
½ tbsp. cinnamon
Salt and pepper to taste
1 tsp. lemon juice
12 chestnuts, peeled and chopped
¾ cup white rice
1 cup water, vegetable, or chicken broth

1. Lightly sauté the green onions, parsley, mint, and garlic until the onions are translucent and the herbs are wilted.
2. Add ground meat, and sauté until browned.
3. Add seasonings and chestnuts to meat mixture. Mix well.
4. Add water or broth. Simmer about 30 minutes, until the liquid is absorbed and the rice is tender.

OPTIONS

♥ Use brown basmati rice instead of white rice. Add 2 cups of water and simmer until rice is tender and liquid is absorbed, approximately 45 minutes to an hour. Add more water, if necessary.
♥ Substitute ground buffalo for round steak.

NOTES

■ To peel chestnuts: Slice chestnuts in half using a sharp knife and remove outer shell. Put in a saucepan, and cover with water. Bring water to boil, and boil for 5 minutes. Remove the pan from heat, and let sit for another 5 minutes. Peel off the loosened inner shell.
■ This "stuffing" never stuffed a chicken or turkey. It's served as a side dish.

CHRISTMAS

At Christmas my family started our celebration at home, waking up very early in the morning to open the presents that Santa brought us the night before. Mom insisted that Stan and I wash our faces and comb our hair before we could come down to the living room, because the first order of business was to take movies of this annual event.

Mom, dressed in a fancy robe and full makeup, directed us, barking out orders: "Okay, Elaine, when you walk down the stairs rub your eyes like you just got up. Now the two of you go over to the fireplace, and Stanton, you look up the chimney to see if Santa got stuck. Don't argue with me! I don't care if you are eleven; it will look cute on film."

My father would stand behind her with a blinding set of camera lights, following the action with his 8-mm movie camera. Only then could we go to the beautifully decorated tree under which were nestled piles of colorfully wrapped presents.

My mother collected delicate glass ornaments when we lived back east. Every year our tree held several surprises: a pink-painted glass hot-air balloon; glass birds that clipped onto the tree branches; or long, jeweled bulbs. She believed in tinsel and bubble lights as well, which made our trees sparkle out our front window into the frosty night. To me those trees were alive and magical. But the magic was short-lived. The year before we moved to California our basement flooded and the collection of ornaments stored there was ruined. Soon after we moved out West, my father decided to modernize. He bought an artificial aluminum tree, which my mother chose to decorate with only dark turquoise glass bulbs, plastic turquoise tassels, and strings of glass turquoise beads. The tree was lit with one rotating spotlight—alternately yellow, red, blue, and green. We were "with it," but Christmas was not quite the same to me after that.

However, Christmas dinners continued to follow tradition and were wonderful. The Thanksgiving turkey was replaced with baked

She believed in tinsel and bubble lights, making our trees sparkle out our window into the frosty night. Those trees were alive and magical.

Family and tree dressed for Christmas, 1957: Elaine, Angela, and Stanton

ELENI'S KOUREMBIETHES—BUTTER TEA COOKIES

Yields 8–10 dozen

Preheat oven 375 degrees

1 lb. unsalted butter
½ cup confectioners sugar
2 egg yolks
⅔ cup blanched almonds, finely chopped
     or 1 tsp. almond extract
1 oz. masticha brandy or whiskey
½ cup orange juice
1 tsp. baking powder
5–5½ cups flour, sifted
Whole cloves (optional)
Sifted confectioners sugar for topping

1. Soften the butter at room temperature, and then cream until very light.
2. Gradually add the sugar, and cream until fluffy and light colored.
3. Beat in the egg yolks, masticha or whiskey, orange juice, and almonds (or almond extract).
4. Sift together the flour and baking powder. Slowly add and blend into creamed ingredients. The dough should be soft but not sticky.
5. Shape into small crescents or 1½ inch balls. Place on greased baking sheets about an inch apart, and stud each cookie with a clove. Bake in a 375-degree oven for 20 minutes or until lightly browned.
6. After taking the cookies out of the oven, sift a fine layer of confectioners' sugar on waxed paper. Place slightly cooled cookies on top of the sugar layer.
7. Liberally sift confectioners' sugar over the tops and sides of the cookies. Cool completely before storing.

NOTES

- Masticha is a specialty brandy from Greece. See Resources.
- I love a clove in my cookie, and it is the traditional ingredient for this recipe. My daughter does not. You may want to omit the cloves if you think your guests would object to the possibility of biting into a small twig with a very strong flavor.

ANGELA'S KOUREMBIETHES—BUTTER TEA COOKIES

Yields 5 dozen

Preheat oven to 350 degrees

1 lb. unsalted butter
½ cup confectioners sugar
2 egg yolks, slightly beaten
¾ cup chopped blanched almonds, browned
1 oz. brandy or whiskey
½ cup orange juice
1 tsp. baking powder
6 cups flour
Whole cloves (optional)
Confectioners sugar for topping

1. Soften the butter at room temperature until very soft. Cream until very light.
2. Gradually beat in the sugar until light and fluffy.
3. Add eggs yolks and beat thoroughly. Mix in the almonds, brandy or whiskey, and orange juice.
4. Sift the baking powder and flour together and gradually blend into the dough.
5. With floured hands, shape dough into 1½ inch balls or into three inch crescents. If desired, stud each piece with a whole clove, driven into its middle.
6. Bake on cookie sheets in a 350-degree oven for 20 minutes or until very lightly browned.
7. Sift confectioner's sugar onto a long sheet of waxed paper. As soon as you remove the cookies from the oven place them on the bed of sugar, and when slightly cooled sift additional sugar liberally on top of the cookies.
8. Cool cookies completely before storing.

We finally went home in our cold and frosty Pontiac or Chevy, our trunk full of our presents and our tummies full of Greek food.

Christmas ham as well as roast leg of lamb. And while the candied yams were still included, *Yaya* Eleni served pilafi with yogurt to accompany the lamb. In Detroit we ate dinner and *baklava* or *galatoboureko* at *Yaya* Eleni's house, followed up by our second helping of dessert from trays of *koulourakia* and *kourembiedes* at *Yaya* Despina's. We greeted each other with *Kala Christouyenna* (Merry Christmas) and collected many more gifts along the way, finally going home in our very cold and frosty Pontiac or Chevy, our trunk full of our presents and our tummies full of Greek food. The dessert I associate with the Christmases of my youth is *Kourembiedes*. This buttery cookie with its thick coating of powdered sugar reminds me of my snowy holidays in the East. Included in this section are two family versions.

NEW YEAR'S AND ST. BASIL'S DAY

Greeks, a superstitious lot, start the New Year seeking good fortune and luck, with coins baked into the Vasilopita. Whoever finds them would have good luck for the coming year.

New Year's Day coincides with the Greek holiday for St. Basil, so our family combined the celebration. On New Year's Day we followed much the same pattern of eating we did at Christmas, a week earlier. We always celebrated at *Yaya* Eleni's house because her son, my Uncle Bill, was named after the saint, thus it was his name day. (Both Basil and Bill, i.e. William, are translated from the Greek, *Vasili*.) Basil was a bishop and saint who lived in the fourth century, a model of Christian virtue and defender of the true faith, but better known to us for the special bread named after him and eaten by the faithful on his saintly celebration day.

In Greece, name days are celebrated instead of birthdays. The name day celebrations are associated with the days designated by the church to honor the saints after whom people are named. For example, those named for Saint Basil celebrate their name day on January 1, St. Basil's Day. My father's, *Yaya* Eleni's, and my name days are on May 21, the day that commemorates Saints Helen (Eleni) and Constantine.

Eleni's Vasilopita and Pascha Kouloures —New Year's and Easter Bread

Yields 4 round loaves, 10 inches in diameter

Preheat oven to 350 degrees

¾ lb. soft butter
2 cups sugar
9 eggs
1½ tsp. salt
1 tsp. masticha (ground into fine powder)
    or ¾ tsp. mahlepi (see Notes)
1 tsp. cinnamon
1 qt. milk (lukewarm)
4 cakes or pkgs. yeast
Approximately 23–25 cups white flour

1. Cream together butter and sugar.
2. Beat the eggs slightly; then add them to the mixture and beat until light.
3. Stir in the spices.
4. Warm milk to lukewarm. Dissolve the yeast in a cup using ¼ cup warmed milk. Add the dissolved yeast, with the rest of the quart of warmed milk, to the butter-sugar-egg mixture. Mix well.
5. Add flour gradually, making sure that each addition is well mixed into the batter before adding more.
6. Add the flour until the dough has a consistency that is ready to knead; that is, it is firm yet pliable, moist but not sticky. Practice will help you to determine the proper consistency.
7. Knead the dough for at least 5 minutes on a floured surface, until the consistency is stretchy and smooth on the outside.
8. Place the dough in a large bowl and cover it with a clean sheet and a wool blanket (an electric blanket set on the lowest setting is also good). Let it rise 1 hour.
9. Knead the dough again; cover and let it rise 1 hour.
10. Knead it a third time and mold into desired shapes (see Notes). Cover and let the loaves rise again until roughly double in size.

Continued on next page

11. Beat 1 egg and brush the liquid on the dough. Sprinkle with sesame seeds and decorate per the season (see Notes).

12. Bake for ½ hour. Switch the breads from 1 rack to the other (i.e., those on the top rack are switched with the ones on the bottom rack). Bake for another 10 minutes, or until bread is a golden brown.

NOTES

- Before baking the New Year's Bread push a well-scrubbed coin into the center of each loaf. We typically put quarters in the larger loaves and dimes in the smaller ones. For those who don't like the bread to be discolored while baking, with oxidation from the coins, wrap each washed coin in aluminum foil before insertion. Whole blanched almonds or halves of walnut meats can be pressed into the tops of the loaves for decoration (about 6 placed around the top of the loaf).

- Traditionally masticha is used for Easter Bread and mahlepi is used for New Year's Bread. (See appendices for an explanation of these spices and their availability.)

- Shapes for Easter bread are either round loaves or a long roll of dough that is folded in half lengthwise and twisted 2 times to form a simple braid. New Year's Bread is always round.

- Easter Bread is decorated by pressing a hard-boiled, red-dyed egg into the center of the round loaves or at the top round of the twist in the braided loaf.

- If you choose to make a half-recipe use 5 eggs.

There were a few differences between Christmas and New Year's celebrations. Instead of wishing everybody *Kala Christouyena* (Merry Christmas) we greeted each other with *Chronia Polla* (literally "many years"). And instead of collecting gifts we collected loaves of *Vasilopita*, the traditional bread dedicated to St. Basil.

Greeks are typically a superstitious lot who like to start the New Year seeking good fortune and better luck. To symbolize the good fortune, coins are baked into each of the *Vasilopita* loaves, and whoever finds the one coin in their loaf will have good luck for the coming year. As we gathered around *Yaya* Eleni's dining room table, I held my breath as each person cut into the big main loaf and took their slice. Was this going to be the slice with the quarter?

Sometimes the knife was passed to me before the coin was found. I would take the knife in my hand and close my eyes, praying for luck. I then would slice into the dense bread hoping to be stopped short when the knife hit the coin. I don't think I ever found the coin in that gathering. The knife would slice through, and I would watch the loaf continue around the table, while I nibbled on the sweet, fresh-baked bread. Since both grandmothers baked their own recipes of this bread, each making a large loaf as well as individual loaves for each person, we all had plenty of bread to bring home and lots of coins and good luck to share.

EASTER

Easter, or *Pascha* as it is called in Greek, was very different from any other holiday my family celebrated—well, not the food but the activities. This was truly our most church-centered holiday. The big excitement for my brother Stanton and me when we were young was accompanying our parents to all the late-night Easter Week services and holding our own lighted candles at the Friday and Saturday night rites.

The most memorable year for us was when Stanton was an altar boy and had to stand stock still, at attention, through several services. We watched as he solemnly stood at the front of the church in his cream-white robe and red sash, almost overcome by the smell of incense and hypnotized by the flame of the candle stuck in a long brass candle holder he held in front of him. My parents and I held our breaths in trepidation as he started swaying, almost losing his balance. He was able to stay the course, however, and later regaled us with his stories of three nights before the altar—his physical discomfort, the valiant attempts he made to keep from fainting or falling asleep, how

My parents and I held our breaths in trepidation as he started swaying, almost losing his balance.

ELENI'S YAOURTI—GREEK-STYLE YOGURT

Yields 9–10 cups

2 qt. milk
1 cup cream or 2 small cans evaporated milk
3 tbsp. previously made yogurt (referred
    to as the starter, see Notes for its
    purpose)

1. Bring milk to boil; simmer for 20
   minutes, stirring constantly to keep it
   from sticking to the bottom of the pan.
2. Add cream or evaporated milk; stir well.
3. Cool the mixture until lukewarm.
4. Thin the yogurt starter in a cup of the
   warmed milk, and then add it to the rest
   of the milk. Blend well.
5. Pour into a large bowl or individual
   molds and cover. Keep the bowl in warm
   place until set and thick. This could take
   from 5 hours to overnight.
6. Refrigerate until served.

OPTIONS

- To halve recipe, use 2 tbsp. yogurt for 1
  qt. milk.
- If you would like a thicker, creamier
  yogurt, place the yogurt in a muslin bag
  and suspend to let excess liquid drain.

NOTES

Here are some things to consider for
successful yogurt making:

- Protect the starter from contamination.
  Do not open the starter (either plain
  yogurt recently purchased from the
  store, or 8-oz. starter from the yogurt
  batch you have previously made and
  sealed in a separate container) until you
  are ready to make the next batch.
- Properly cleanse and heat-treat your
  containers, to keep out unwanted
  bacteria. Washing the containers in
  a dishwasher would be the most
  convenient way to do this, or sterilize
  the containers by submerging them in
  boiling water for 20 minutes.
- The proper incubation temperature
  for the Lactobacillus (the bacteria that
  produces yogurt) is between 98°F
  (37°C) and 130° F (55°C). Anything
  below that range does not grow well;
  anything above will kill the bacteria. An

Continued on next page

incubation temperature of 122°F (50°C) is preferred, because it will inhibit the growth of unwanted bacteria.

- Yogurt is preserved by its acidity, which inhibits the growth of unwanted bacteria. With container lids on tight, this yogurt will keep at least a month or 2 in the refrigerator.

Information from http://biology.clc.uc.edu/fankhauser/Cheese/yogurt_making/YOGURT2000.htm

much his feet and back hurt. (Oh, was there a spiritually uplifting church service happening along with all of his heroics?)

In Detroit, our family—the Manolakas and Vlisides aunts, uncles, and cousins—all went to St. Nicholas Church, so we saw them every night of Holy Week. My Aunt Ginny directed the choir and my mother sang soprano. My father and his Uncles, Jim and Steve, being on the parish council, served as ushers, and the rest of the family— *Yaya* Despina, my great aunts, and second cousins lined the pews. After the long candle-lit midnight liturgy on Saturday we met them outside the church to wish them *Christos Anesti* (Christ Is Risen). They responded to us with *Alithos Anesti* (Truly He Has Risen). Then we hurried home for a feast my mother had prepared to break the Lenten fast, a meal featuring the meat, fish, cheese, and eggs that we had forgone the six weeks before.

When we woke up late on Easter morning we made the family rounds, the same as every holiday. But during dinner, we cracked the ends of our deep red Easter eggs against each other, repeating *Christos Anesti*. Each time one of the egg ends would break, making the owner of the hardest, unbroken egg the winner of that round. The egg cracking rounds continued until someone's egg had withstood all the cracks and bashes, making that person champion. We came home Easter night full

The egg cracking rounds continued until someone's egg had withstood all the cracks and bashes, making that person champion.

Aunt Kathryn and Uncle Don
preparing for their Easter feast, 2002

*I heard my aunt sing
the Lamentations. The
beauty of her voice
transported me.*

of delicious lamb, rice pilaf, and Yaya Eleni's homemade yogurt and carried with us many cracked eggs and loaves of Easter bread.

Easter bread is similar to New Year's *Vasilopita*, except instead of coins, we press hard cooked, red-dyed eggs into the tops of the loaves before baking. (See page 83 for **Eleni's Easter Bread** recipe.)

A DETROIT EASTER REVISITED

In 2002, I returned to Detroit to visit Aunt Kathryn (my mother's younger sister) and her family for the Easter celebration. My mission was to learn how to make some of her notable recipes. Aunt Kathryn and Uncle Don attended the big cathedral that had been built on the site of my mother's old neighborhood church and Greek school. Worshiping in the same neighborhood where my mother had grown up was very nourishing to my soul.

The most fulfilling religious experience was Good Friday service, which included two remarkable events. The first happened during a long hymn the choir sings only during this service, once a year. It is called the "Lamentations," referring to a series of laments of the myrrh-bearing women who went to visit Christ's body in the tomb. I joined my aunt and uncle in the choir loft, because true to family tradition, I also sang in my church choir.

Aunt Kathryn was blessed with the best voice in the family. She had studied opera before she married Uncle Don, so she was given the long solo in the Lamentations to sing every year. That year was the first time I heard my aunt sing it. As I sat beside her in the soprano section and listened to her, the beauty of her voice transported me. It truly sounded like an angel's. I was proud to be her niece.

The other profound experience that day was the ritual reenactment of Christ's funeral procession, which each Greek Orthodox Church performs on Good Friday. The tradition my mother's old church followed, and this cathedral continues, includes the whole congregation

KATHRYN'S TARAMASALATA—FISH ROE DIP

4-oz. jar of *tarama*
¼ cup onion, finely grated
¾–1 cup olive oil
6 slices sweet French bread, crusts
   trimmed
Juice of 2 lemons

1. Moisten bread with water until it is soft and can be formed into a ball; squeeze out the excess water.
2. Put moistened bread and *tarama* into a blender. Process on medium speed.
3. Keep the blender going as you add onions, juice, and then slowly pour in the olive oil.
4. Continue to blend until smooth and creamy.

OPTION

If you use a food processor, there is no need to grate the onions. Chop them fine and add them in with the juice and oil. They will become finely grated.

walking behind Christ's bier through the surrounding neighborhood. As we exited the cathedral I noticed policemen placed along the route to stop traffic for us and keep the way clear. As we turned the corner of the cathedral property and passed along the side of it, the Greektown gambling casino was on our left. Patrons entering the casino stared at us with a mixture of confusion and awe. Further along, on our right, was the Catholic Church. All the Catholic parishioners had paused their Good Friday service and stood on the steps of their church to watch our procession as it passed. Standing silently reverent, they crossed themselves as our Lord's bier was carried by.

We then turned onto Monroe Avenue, crowded with Greek restaurants and coffeehouses, tourists and diners. Crowds lined the parade route, and on their faces I saw assorted expressions—respect, annoyance, awe, confusion, impatience, disbelief. Several Greek waiters were allowed to leave their posts and watch the procession as it passed their restaurants. They did their cross when Christ's bier passed, before disappearing back inside to serve their patrons.

Cousins Jonathan and Kathy with Elaine at the 2002 Easter feast

My mother had told me about the many bachelors and husbands, whose families had not yet immigrated, who congregated each night in the coffee houses and tavernas, to drink, socialize, and play cards. She also described this procession when she was a child. Good Friday was the same as every night for these men, except for one difference. As the bier of Christ passed, the men would leave their card games, light a candle, and, like the waiters I saw, go out to the street to watch the procession. They would cross themselves as the bier passed in front of them, and when it continued on, they would go back to their card games and drinks.

I was very proud to be a part of the procession and to be singing in the choir. The clergy's, choir's, and congregation's voices resounded against the close buildings, making solemn and beautiful music. The majesty and significance of the ceremony of which I was a part created awe in the bystanders. But my thoughts about the ornate ceremony of the bishop and his entourage were jumbled as we wound through a section of town that had been invaded by big business and a multitude of tourists. I imagined I was part of a Posada in Mexico, taking the church relics through the crowded village plaza, except instead of understanding and worship, strangers who did not comprehend the occasion and the ceremony surrounded us. Simultaneously, I felt I had entered my mother's existence; I was seeing the world and

Kathryn's Spanakopita—Spinach Pie

Yields 12 3-inch square servings

Preheat oven 350 degrees

⅓ cup olive oil
¼ lb. combined butter and margarine
¾–1 cup finely chopped leeks (white
    part only)
1½ cup chopped fresh parsley
½ cup chopped fresh dill or 1½ tbsp.
    dry dill
½ tsp. oregano
2 lbs. chopped fresh spinach or 2 10-oz.
    pkgs. frozen chopped spinach
7 large or 8 medium eggs, beaten
1 lb. feta cheese, crumbled
1 lb. ricotta or fine cottage cheese
⅛ tsp. white pepper
¾–1 tsp. salt
¾ lb. butter and margarine
1 pkg. phyllo dough

1. Melt ¼ lb. of the butter/margarine
   mixture and ⅓ cup oil in a large
   frying pan; add leeks and herbs and
   sauté slightly.

2. Steam the fresh spinach or cook
   the frozen according to the package
   directions. Drain and dry the spinach
   (squeeze all the water out of it). Mix
   it with the herbs and leeks; then
   take the pan off the heat. Mix all the
   ingredients (except the rest of the
   butter/margarine and phyllo) one at a
   time into the sautéed leeks and herbs,
   blending thoroughly after each addition.

3. Place one at a time, half of the layers of
   phyllo pastry sheets in an oiled 10 x 15
   x 2 inch pan, brushing each sheet well
   with melted butter. (Refrigerate half of
   the sheets while using up the first half.
   The sheets that you are using should be
   kept in a dampened towel.)

4. Add ½ the spinach mixture and place
   1 sheet of phyllo pastry on top of it (no
   butter). Add the last half of the spinach
   mixture.

5. Place one at a time, the rest of the
   layers of phyllo pastry sheets on the
   filling, again buttering each sheet. Score

Continued on next page

the top layers with a sharp knife for the squares you will be cutting it into after baking.

6. Bake at 350 degrees about 1 hour or more, until browned. (But check after 45 minutes.) Cut into small squares before serving.

7. If you want to freeze the dish for later serving, score the top of the phyllo for the squares you will cut it into after baking. To serve, put into the oven frozen and bake for 1 hour and 45 minutes at 350 degrees.

An ecstatic moment of heightened awareness and flow—a merging of ancient and modern, of physical and transcendent worlds, beyond time.

neighborhood through her eyes, however transformed it had become. She was with me in spirit that night, walking down the streets by the home of her birth.

That feeling became very strong as we approached the back of the church property. We walked right in front of where her house used to be, just across the street from the church itself. I wondered, where had it actually stood? Where would my grandfather's snack shack have been? What had the neighborhood looked like then? My head was spinning with these thoughts and questions, but it didn't take me out of the moment. Instead, it amplified my physical sensations. For me it was an ecstatic moment of heightened awareness and flow, between time, place, and cultures—a merging of the ancient and modern, of physical and transcendent worlds, beyond time.

I was sad when it ended. I could have gone around the church at least one more time, prolonging these feelings and remembering the stories my mother had shared with me about her Easters there.

On Easter Sunday, my week-long apprenticeship in my aunt's kitchen paid off. My cousins and their wives and families joined us for the gourmet Greek feast my aunt, uncle, and I served. The *taramasalata* was tart and creamy. The roast leg of lamb was rich and juicy. And the

Kathryn's Galatoboureko

Serves 24

Preheat oven 350 degrees

Custard and Crust

1 qt. milk
1¾ cup sugar
¾ cup "Cream of Wheat"
½ lb. butter or margarine
10 eggs, separated
2 tsp. orange rind
1 tsp. vanilla
¼ cup brandy or peach liqueur
    (optional)
Cinnamon
1 lb. phyllo dough
½ lb. butter or margarine, melted

Syrup

3½ cups sugar
2½ cups boiling water
1 tsp. lemon juice
1 cinnamon stick (optional)

1. Combine the syrup ingredients in a saucepan. Bring to boil, and simmer for 15 minutes. Cool.

Galatoboureko: Delicate and flavorful custard, surrounded with crisp phyllo and drenched in a honeyed syrup

2. Heat milk and ½ the sugar in a saucepan over a low heat until warm. Add "Cream of Wheat" gradually, stirring constantly until it is thickened and smooth.

3. Add butter, and stir until its melted. Remove from heat.

4. Stir in vanilla, orange rind, and brandy or liqueur. Allow mixture to cool.

5. Butter a 11 x 15 x 2 inch pan with melted butter or margarine. Brushing

Continued on next page

each phyllo sheet first with melted butter, layer half the sheets, one at a time, into pan. (The phyllo should be kept in a dampened towel until it's used. Refrigerate the other half of the sheets until needed.)

6. Beat egg whites until stiff. Beat egg yolks and remaining sugar until it becomes a light yellow, creamy batter about three times the original volume; fold them into the whites. Stir in the cooled milk mixture.

7. Pour this resulting mixture on top of the buttered sheets. Layer the remaining half of the phyllo, brushing each sheet with melted butter.

8. With a sharp knife, cut top pastry into 4 or 5 strips across the length of the pan.

9. Bake in a preheated 350-degree oven for an hour, until top is lightly browned.

10. When the custard has finished baking, remove from the oven and pour COOL syrup over the hot galatoboureko. Cool, and then cut into squares before serving. Do not cover the pan or it will make the dessert soggy.

galatoboureko was the best I ever tasted. After it was all over and our guests left for home, I ordered my aunt and uncle to go into the living room to relax. It took me four hours to clean up the kitchen, even with the help I finally accepted from my uncle when he offered to dry some of the pots and pans. The wonderful meal was worth the days of preparation and my dishpan hands. Here are the recipes I learned on that memorable visit.

When we moved to California many things changed about our holidays. We watched the Thanksgiving parades on the television. During our first Christmas Day in Los Angeles we went swimming in Uncle Lee and Aunt Chubby's swimming pool, which was unimaginable in Detroit. My parents sang the Easter services in the prestigious St. Sophia Cathedral Choir in Los Angeles, and when my brother and I were in our teens, we joined them. On Easter Day we met friends and family at the church picnic instead of at my grandmothers' houses. My

KATHRYN'S KOULOURAKIA

Yields 45–50 cookies

Preheat oven to 350 degrees

3 sticks unsalted butter, softened
1 cup sugar
3 eggs
1½ tsp. vanilla
4½ cup flour
3 tsp. baking powder
⅛ tsp. salt

1 egg, beaten
3 tbsp. water
Sesame seeds

1. Cream butter and sugar together.
2. Beat in eggs and vanilla.
3. Sift together flour, baking powder, and salt.
4. Slowly mix in flour mixture to the creamed mixture.
5. Chill dough in refrigerator for 1 hour or stiff and easy to handle.
6. Roll into snakes of various lengths, about ½ inch in diameter, and then form into different *koulourakia* shapes: e.g. circles, 3-inch lengths, 6-inch lengths doubled lengthwise, 6-inch lengths doubled lengthwise and twisted into a simple braid, spirals. (Use about 2–3 tbsp. of dough to form each of the shapes.) Yield depends on size and shape of cookies.
7. Beat the water into the beaten egg and brush onto the cookies; sprinkle with sesame seeds.
8. Bake on greased cookie sheets for 20–25 minutes, until golden brown.

Greek Salad: fresh greens and vegetables, dressed with feta and a vinaigrette

My Mother's California Kitchen

EVERYDAY FARE

Many of the memories I have shared in this book have been about celebrations and holidays. Yes, the Greeks love to party, particularly my family. But most nights we ate at home, just my mother and father, my brother Stanton, and me. We lived in Detroit through the 1950s, where we sat on modernistic wooden chairs around the small, rectangular, laminated imitation wood top of a kitchen table, looking out at the seasons from our bay window. In the fall bronzed leaves scuttled across the driveway; in winter our back yard was

A Manolakas gathering, fall 1963, Connie and Angie's house

blanketed in pristine white snow; and in the spring bushes of lilacs and forsythias stood among a carpet of delicate lilies of the valley. It was our nightly ritual to gather for dinner, uninterrupted by the television, radio, or telephone calls. We didn't have to talk to each other, but we were expected to be there and to eat.

We had to clean our plates, while my mother repeated that era's mealtime refrain, "Remember the starving children in China."

Growing up, Stanton and I had to clean our plates, while my mother repeated that era's mealtime refrain, "Remember the starving children in China." If perchance that sad specter didn't work on us, we were made to sit at the table until everything on our plates was gone. My brother never had any trouble finishing his meals, but those were the years I picked at my food. At holiday dinners, while my brother and cousins would shovel their food into their maws, Aunt Kathryn would shake her head and say to me, "You eat like a bird." So I stayed late at the table many evenings while everybody else had finished their meals and left. I would push the food around my plate with my fork hoping that if I changed the placement of the remains, I could fool my mother into thinking I had eaten more.

While I sat there, wasting the food that could save the poor of the world, my mother finished washing the dishes, except for my plate and fork. Her strategy never worked. Although I fooled nobody, I was finally excused after executing my mother's desperate demand to, "Eat one more bite," and to dry the silverware, which was my clean-up task as a little girl. Somehow I managed to grow to a more than healthy weight, regardless of the hamburger or spinach or macaroni I left uneaten throughout those years.

When we moved to California the only things that changed were the shape of the kitchen table and my responsibilities for cleaning up after dinner. Now we sat on metal chairs with padded plastic covered seats, at a crowded brown Formica bar attached to our kitchen counter. Our fine view was now of our kitchen sink full of the pots and pans we had used to prepare dinner. My mother found a job as a secretary at the local school district after we moved, so I cleaned the entire kitchen every night.

We were a very traditional Greek family in terms of household duties. As a female I had KP duty as well as helping my mother cook, clean the house, and do the laundry every week. As the male heir, Stanton's one and only job was to mow the lawn two or three times a

ELENI'S YOUVARLAKIA—MEATBALLS WITH EGG/LEMON SAUCE

Yields 6 servings

1½ lb. ground meat
⅓ cup rice
1 egg, slightly beaten
1 clove garlic, minced
2 tbsp. chopped fresh parsley
1½ to 2 tbsp. chopped fresh dill or 1–2 tsp.
   dry dill (see note)
½ tsp. salt and ¼ tsp. pepper
⅓ cup flour
2¼ cups boiling chicken broth or bouillon

SAUCE

2 eggs
Juice of 1 lemon

1. In a bowl combine meat, rice, 1 egg, garlic, parsley, dill, salt, pepper; mix well.
2. With floured hands, shape the mixture into walnut-sized balls. Roll them lightly in flour, shaking off the excess.
3. Place meatballs in a 4-quart pot. Pour boiling chicken broth to cover. Simmer, covered, for 45 minutes.
4. Remove meatballs from pot into a serving dish. Cover to keep warm.
5. Add more liquid to make 1 cup in the pot; boil for 2–3 minutes. Remove from heat.
6. Beat eggs until frothy. Slowly add the lemon juice, beating all the while.
7. Add 1 cup pot liquid slowly to egg mixture, beating constantly, or the egg will congeal. Place meatballs into sauce and stir gently to combine. Heat over very low heat until gravy thickens. Serve.

OPTIONS

- Use beef, veal, or lamb. For a leaner option use ground buffalo meat.
- Substitute brown basmati rice for white rice. Parboil for 10 minutes before adding to the meat mixture.

NOTE

The original recipe calls for 1½ to 2 tbsp. fresh or 1–2 tsp. dry dill. My family prefers it with the lesser amount.

ANGELA'S GREEK SIDE DISH PASTA

Yields 4–6 servings

1-lb. pkg. of spaghetti or pasta
¼ cup butter
2 cloves garlic, minced
½ cup grated mizithra, Parmesan, or
   Romano cheese

1. Prepare the spaghetti or pasta according to the instructions on the package.
2. After the spaghetti is cooked, rinse and drain it in a colander.
3. Melt the butter in a large pan. Over medium-low heat, sauté the garlic in the butter until the garlic is soft and golden, and butter has browned.
4. Pour the drained spaghetti or pasta into the pan of butter and toss to coat.
5. Stir in the shredded cheese and serve.

month. My father did help me out, however. Until I graduated from high school, he taught me how to sweep the kitchen floor, *every night*. His style of sweeping was distinguished by brisk, energetic brush strokes, as if to punish the dust for alighting on our floor. My style called for a languorous, more thoughtful stroke that didn't meet his bustling standards.

During those homey nights my mother still fed us excellent and varied menus of basic ingredients, driven by what was either on sale or discounted by the many coupons my father clipped. (We ate a lot of *Campbell's* chicken noodle soup and *Vons* fresh peach ice cream in those days, because of my father's economy.) The preparation was also sometimes faster and simpler.

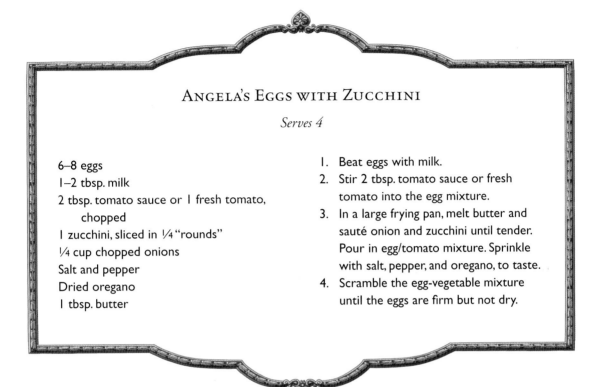

ANGELA'S EGGS WITH ZUCCHINI

Serves 4

6–8 eggs
1–2 tbsp. milk
2 tbsp. tomato sauce or 1 fresh tomato,
    chopped
1 zucchini, sliced in ¼ "rounds"
¼ cup chopped onions
Salt and pepper
Dried oregano
1 tbsp. butter

1. Beat eggs with milk.
2. Stir 2 tbsp. tomato sauce or fresh tomato into the egg mixture.
3. In a large frying pan, melt butter and sauté onion and zucchini until tender. Pour in egg/tomato mixture. Sprinkle with salt, pepper, and oregano, to taste.
4. Scramble the egg-vegetable mixture until the eggs are firm but not dry.

I carried all of those basic recipes with me into adulthood and to my own family. I still cherish them as distinctive of my mother's Greek style of cooking. How many other people broil their calf's liver, seasoned with lemon and oregano? How many serve their families a side dish of spaghetti, sauced with garlic, browned butter, and mizithra cheese? Even the omelets my mother devised were kissed with the Greek touch. And there are those recipes, such as *Youvarlakia*, my mother had carried to her home from *Yaya* Eleni's, which contained my grandmother's hallmarks of hearty and tasty. Many of the recipes in other parts of this book were also daily standards: Greek salad, dandelion greens, the baked chicken recipes, and my grandfather's hamburgers.

"Gather for dinner every night; turn off the TV; and cook from scratch these delicious and nourishing meals."

Connie Manolakas at the helm

My father heard the call of the sea. Though he was a draftsman, he was born to sail.

If I could change just one thing about modern life, I would change the way the modern family eats dinner. I say, "Gather for dinner every night; turn off the TV; and cook from scratch these delicious and nourishing meals."

MY DAD THE SAILOR

The following recipe became a steady entrée in our family cuisine during the 1960s, when we regularly went deep-sea fishing and brought home a lot of catch. Not long after we moved to Whittier, California, my parents became life-long friends with Mary and Bob Winders. Mary's maiden name was Mavrakis; her family was Cretan, like *Yaya* Eleni's. That was enough to forge a strong bond between my mother and Mary. Mary was also a social animal, like my parents, and a real glamour queen. Until the day she died in her mid-seventies, she wore an elaborately coiffed platinum blond wig and dripped with enough jewels to have made Marie Antoinette jealous. Mary dabbled in Japanese importing, which made her a reliable supplier of jade jewelry, strange Asian inventions (including a bowling ball with a retractable handle instead of finger-holes), and a parade of fascinating Japanese business associates who communicated to us in Pidgin English.

Bob Winders was an engineer who invented machinery to manufacture box-spring mattresses and owned a mattress factory in East Los Angeles. He also owned a series of cabin cruisers. This sealed the friendship for my father, who was an avid seaman. Because Bob liked to fiddle with the motor more than pilot the boat and my father loved to take the helm, they made a perfect team. Our family would spend weekends and holidays sailing their boat along the Pacific shore. Early in the morning we would leave for a day of fishing, returning to dock at night just off Balboa Island in Newport, where we would sleep in the boat's many bunks.

As I have mentioned, the Manolakas family's traditional occupation on the island of Chios was seafaring. *Papou* Stamatios was a captain before he decided to come to America. In the 1920s, after he had made his "fortune," the family returned to Chios, Greece, for several years, where my grandfather literally took his place at the helm in the family business. But Sam didn't have the sea in his blood, and he missed his family too much on the long voyages across the Mediterranean, so the family returned to America and started the Brown Cow restaurant. But my father still heard the call of the sea. Though he earned his keep as a draftsman, working in an office bent over a drafting table for too many hours a week, he was born to sail.

During the years we summered at our cottage in Canada, he took a pilot's class and owned two sailboats and a motorboat. The first sailboat sank at its mooring during a fierce storm before I was born, when a rare hurricane blew into the Great Lakes region. However, when I was a child I spent many hours sailing with my father on Lake St. Clair in its successor. Usually, after he came home from work, we would glide our sailboat over calm lake waters as the setting sun splashed reds, pinks, and purples across the sky. Or during long weekend days we would cruise the narrow Belle River in the motorboat, through verdant farm country and quaint villages.

My father was in seventh heaven driving the various yachts that Bob owned and sailed on the California coast. While my father captained the cruisers, the rest of the guests fished. We caught a fair amount of tuna and red snapper, but mostly our catch were sharks (which we threw back) and barracuda, an oily fish with a very strong flavor.

I thought my parents made better use of the barracuda when they buried it under their citrus trees—old country fertilizer. It grew

We'd glide our sailboat over calm lake waters as the setting sun splashed reds, pinks, and purples across the sky, or cruise Belle River in the motorboat, through farm country and villages.

PSARI PLAKI—BAKED FISH WITH VEGETABLES

Yields 4–6 servings

Preheat oven 350 degrees

Up to 3 lbs. fish (use sole,
    cod, snapper, or trout)
Salt and pepper, to taste
Dried oregano, to taste
½ cup olive oil
3 fresh tomatoes, chopped
    or 1 14½ oz. can diced
    tomatoes
2 bunches green onions,
    finely sliced
½ cup chopped green
    pepper
1 cup parsley, chopped
1 or 2 cloves garlic, minced
1–2 tbsp. butter
Garnish: raw onion rings and lemon slices

Colorful vegetables enhance the flavor of the fish

1. Place the fish in greased baking pan.
2. Sprinkle it with salt, pepper, and oregano.
3. Pour olive oil evenly on top of the fish.
4. Spread a mixture of tomatoes, onions,
    parsley, garlic, and green pepper on top
    of the fish.
5. Dot with butter and decorate with
    onion rings and lemon slices.
6. Bake for 30–40 minutes or until the fish
    is cooked through.

OPTIONS

♥ Vegetable broth can replace olive oil for
a low fat option.

great crops of oranges and lemons unless our dog, Shaggy, dug up the fish before they decomposed. We could immediately tell when that happened—the smell was hellacious. It always earned Shaggy, a mutt who resembled a miniature version of Disney's "The Shaggy Dog," an immediate trip to the dog-groomers, where she was shampooed and sheared of her thick, wooly coat. With the loss of that coat, Shaggy must have felt naked and ashamed. She would slink around with her head down and pain in her eyes, for at least a week after the shearing.

My mother's spicy tomato recipe, Psari Plaki, even tamed the fishy taste of the barracuda. It is a very healthy and delicious fish dish, especially when made with sole, cod, or snapper.

I fell asleep with the incense of Uncle George's cigar smoke and the loud lullaby, "Connie, stop looking at my cards."

ANGELA'S ENTERTAINING

The Carlos conviviality followed my mother into her marriage. My parents entertained several times a month throughout the 55 years of their life together. In California, they would sometimes have my aunts and uncles over for bridge during the week. They would eat, visit, eat, play cards until very late, eat, and accuse each other of cheating. As a teenager I somehow found their raucous behavior comforting. I would fall asleep with the incense of Uncle George Manolakas' cigar smoke and the loud lullaby of, "Connie, stop looking at my cards."

"Are you accusing me of cheating, Lee? Huh! You're just mad because you're losing again."

"Hey, Angie, can you bring me more of that baklava and another cup of coffee?"

Or my parents would have their friends and co-workers over for dinner or parties. Their best friends in California, Mary and Bob Winders, would visit with an entourage of Mary's

Cousin Mary with Angela in her kitchen ready to entertain, circa 1990

ANGELA'S TARAMASALATA—FISH ROE DIP

Yields 1½ to 2 cups

⅓ cup *tarama*
¼–⅓ cup onion, finely grated
I cup olive oil
4–5 slices white bread, crusts trimmed
Juice of 2 or 3 lemons

1. Mash together *tarama* and grated onion.
2. Add a little of the olive oil and beat thoroughly to a smooth paste.
3. Moisten bread and squeeze out excess water.
4. Continue beating *tarama* mixture, adding alternately small bits of moistened bread, olive oil, and lemon juice. Beat until cream-colored.
5. Garnish with a thin slice of lemon or a sprig of parsley. Serve as a dip with crackers or spread on melba toast.

OPTIONS

- ♥ For a dip with less fat, cut olive oil to ½ cup
- Use blender or food processor for ease in mixing and blending ingredients together.
- Any leftover *taramasalata* may be used as dressing for tossed salad.

family or their many Japanese business associates. For those occasions my mother would be deep into food preparation for at least two days prior to the event. Bewildered by the amount of food she planned to serve, I would ask, "What army are you cooking for?" The menu always featured appetizers, typically crackers and cheese, her tart and tasty *Tarama Salata*, and if we were lucky, *Tiropites*.

ANGELA'S ZUCCHINI CASSEROLE

Yields 6 servings

Preheat oven 375 degrees

4–5 zucchinis, sliced into ¼–½ inch
    circles
2 cup onions, halved and sliced
½ cup sliced green and red bell peppers
¼ cup olive oil
2–3 cloves garlic, chopped
½ tsp. salt
¼ tsp. pepper
¼ cup parsley or 1 tsp. dried oregano
¼ tsp. dried dill or mint
1 14½-oz. can stewed tomatoes
1 cup flour
½ cup crumbled feta cheese

1. Sauté the zucchini, onions, and peppers together in the olive oil until slightly soft and coated with oil. Add garlic and sauté until garlic is soft.
2. Add the spices and stewed tomatoes, and simmer for 10–15 minutes.
3. Pour the vegetable mixture into a medium casserole dish, and sprinkle flour over the top.
4. Sprinkle the feta cheese over the floured top, and bake in a 375-degree oven for 30–40 minutes.

A buffet dinner followed the appetizers. My mother cooked two meats—the omnipresent lamb and a poultry dish, accompanied by roast potatoes or pilaf, a casserole like *Moussaka* or *Pastitsio*, and vegetables—perhaps a *Spanakopita*, a fresh Greek Salad, and Greek bread, feta, and olives. Dessert included at least one Greek dessert, most likely Yaya Eleni's secret cookie recipe.

ANGELA'S TOURLOU—ROASTED VEGETABLES

Yields 10–12 servings

Preheat oven 450 degrees

¾ lb. fresh or 1 box frozen green beans
1½ cup fresh or 1 box frozen broccoli
    pieces
2 large potatoes, peeled and cut in pieces
2 medium zucchini, sliced
½ cup chopped celery
1½–2 cups cauliflower pieces
2 large onions, quartered and sliced
3–6 cloves garlic, minced
2 tbsp. olive oil
Salt and pepper to taste
¼ cup chopped fresh parsley
2 tsp. dried dill
1 lb. tomatoes, fresh or canned
Boiling water
½ cup olive oil

1. Arrange the green beans, broccoli, potatoes, zucchini, celery, and cauliflower in a large baking pan.
2. Sauté the onions and garlic in 2 tbsp. olive oil until soft. Pour them over and around the vegetables.
3. Sprinkle salt, pepper, parsley, and dill over the top of the vegetables.
4. Dump the tomatoes onto the dish, and pour enough boiling water over the vegetables to cover the bottom of the pan with 1½ inches of liquid. Then pour ½ cup olive oil over the mix.
5. Cover and bake at 450 degrees until the liquid starts to simmer. Then lower the temperature to 350 degrees, and bake until almost done—approximately 1½ hours.
6. Uncover the pan, and bake on the top rack of the oven until the vegetables are tender and slightly browned.

OPTIONS

- Okra can be substituted for the broccoli. Add either ½ lb. fresh or 1 box frozen okra.
- Carrots, cut into large chunks, are also a good addition to the assorted vegetables.

ANGELA'S SPANAKOPITA—SPINACH PIE

Yields 20 3-inch square servings

Preheat oven 350 degrees

¼ lb. butter or margarine
⅓ cup olive oil
4 bunches green onions
1 large yellow onion, chopped
1½ cup parsley
1½ tbsp. dry dill
½ tsp. oregano
2 10-oz. pkgs. frozen spinach
8 eggs, beaten
1 lb. feta cheese, chopped
1 lb. ricotta or fine cottage cheese
⅛ tsp. white pepper
¾ lb. butter or margarine, melted
1 pkg. phyllo dough

1. Melt ¼ lb. butter; add ⅓ cup olive oil, onions, and herbs, and sauté slightly. Remove from heat.
2. Thaw and drain the spinach. Add it and all the other ingredients (except the rest of the butter and phyllo) one at a time into the onion and herb sauté, blending thoroughly each time. Set aside.

Spanakopita: Spinach laced with herbs, spices, and cheese between two layers of buttery phyllo

3. Brown 3 sheets of the phyllo dough in the oven, and set aside.
4. Brush the bottom of the pan with melted butter. Place 8 layers of phyllo pastry sheets in an 11 x 14 x 2 inch pan, brushing each sheet well with melted butter. (Refrigerate half of the sheets while using up the first half. The sheets that you are using should be kept in a dampened towel.)

Continued on next page

5. Place 1 browned sheet of phyllo pastry on top of the last buttered sheet. Add ½ the spinach mixture; then place the second browned sheet on to of the mixture. Add the last half of the spinach mixture, and top with the third browned sheet.

6. Place 10 layers of phyllo pastry sheets on top of the filling, again buttering each sheet.

7. Cut only the top sheets into 3-inch squares. Bake at 350 degrees 1 hour or more, until browned. (Check after 45 minutes.) Cool and cut through the pieces before serving.

8. If you want to freeze the dish for later serving, score the top of the phyllo for the squares you will cut it into after baking, and freeze. Put it into the oven frozen, and bake for 1 hour, 45 minutes.

My parents' friends had hearty appetites, so they made it all the way through dessert taking large helpings and going back for seconds. But even then, barely a dent was made in the available fare. Much of the abundance went out the door with the guests, on paper plates covered by plastic wrap. Pa, Stan, and I were still assured several days of delicious leftovers.

Even our dog, Shaggy, ate well at these major events. At one of my mother's big shindigs several young guests mistakenly gave the dog all of the chicken that was left. Delicious even to her, Shaggy ate it all and then, literally, didn't move for the next two days.

When my brother Stan and I grew up and moved to our own homes, we made sure we were on hand at those marvelous parties. My mother hosted family events from my children's baptisms to her last triumph, my daughter Sally's engagement party. The next time you entertain you might want to add one or more of these delicacies to your menu. Your guests will love them.

ANGELA'S MOUSSAKA—EGGPLANT CASSEROLE

Serves 12

Preheat oven to 350 degrees

2 medium to large eggplants
Olive oil
1½ lb. ground meat
2 onions, chopped
5 tbsp. butter
1 tbsp. tomato paste
Dash cinnamon
Salt and pepper
¼ cup bread crumbs
4 small zucchinis, sliced lengthwise, no
    more than ¼ inch thick
4 medium potatoes, peeled and sliced
    lengthwise, no more than ¼ inch
    thick
Butter
½ cup water
Grated Parmesan or Romano cheese

TOPPING

6 tbsp. butter
¾ cup flour
1 qt. hot milk
6 eggs

1. Slice eggplant into ½ inch slices and
   sprinkle with salt. Place in a colander
   under a heavy plate for several hours in
   order to press out moisture from the
   eggplant.
2. Brush slices with olive oil and broil
   lightly.
3. Sauté beef and onions in 5 tbsp. butter
   until browned.
4. Add tomato paste, cinnamon, and salt
   and pepper to taste, and mix well.
5. Sprinkle the bottom of a greased large
   baking dish with breadcrumbs. On top
   of the breadcrumbs, alternate layers
   in the following order: sliced eggplant,
   ground meat, zucchini, potatoes, and
   cheese (ending with a top layer of
   eggplant).
6. Dot with butter and add water. Set
   aside.
7. Topping:
   - Melt butter in saucepan. Gradually add
     flour and cook, stirring constantly until
     well mixed and beginning to brown.

Continued on next page

- Heat milk to a simmer. Beat the eggs well, and slowly add the hot milk into the beaten eggs, continuing to beat the eggs to keep them from congealing.
- Slowly add the egg and milk mixture to the browned flour, taking care to mix the thick flour mixture completely into the liquid. Cook over low heat until the mixture is slightly thickened.

8. Pour more than half the sauce on top of the meat and vegetable mixture, and bake in a 350-degree oven for 10 minutes.
9. While waiting for that to bake, return the rest of the sauce to low heat and cook until thick.
10. Pour the thickened sauce onto the top of the casserole, and sprinkle with grated cheese.

11. Continue to bake for 45 or 50 minutes more (until browned).

NOTES

- ♥ Ground beef can be used for the meat. Or for a leaner choice use buffalo. I have also used crumbled soy when I'm cooking for a vegetarian crowd. I use the equivalent amount to the ground meat and add 3 tbsp. of olive oil.
- The original recipe calls for 1 tbsp. of tomato paste. I add 2 tbsp. to mine.
- A "dash" of cinnamon is less than $\frac{1}{8}$ tsp. A little of it goes a long way in meat dishes.

SUNDAY LUNCH

Every Sunday from the time I was ten until I left my parents' home for college, we would wake up early in order to get to church on time. "On time" for my father meant at least fifteen minutes early. (Evidently Pa never subscribed to the notion of "Greek time," the common practice of always showing up a half-hour to an hour late.) When we moved to California, we attended St. Sophia Greek Orthodox Cathedral in downtown Los Angeles, a good half-hour by freeway from our home. Church started at ten-thirty in the morning, which meant that we had to be out the door by nine forty-five. Always my father was in the car by nine thirty-five, impatiently honking the horn as I searched for my hat and gloves, both of which my mother insisted that I wear. And I would complain to anyone who would listen that we weren't late, so why did he have to wake up the neighborhood by honking at us to hurry.

For more than 40 years my parents attended St. Sophia Cathedral, a landmark in Los Angeles built by movie mogul Charles P. Skouros, circa 1950. It is an enormous and fabulously ornate edifice. Its large altar area is faced with lustrous marble, and the tall gate across the broad expanse of the altar, called the *iconstasis*, is decorated with life-sized icons and gold leaf. Colorful murals and more gold leaf deck the walls and ceilings, all depicting saints or scenes from the life of Christ. Christ stares down at the faithful from the expansive dome, his hand upraised, eternally blessing the congregation. Mammoth crystal chandeliers hang from the ceilings, and the acoustics magnify the sounds of the euphonious organ and the 40-voice choir. Organ and singers are situated in the choir loft, which is elevated across the entire back wall of the cathedral. People come from around the world to visit the cathedral and gain inspiration from its beauty.

Because my father was a fast and crazy driver, we made it to this landmark in twenty-five minutes, getting there a full twenty minutes before the service started. My parents went up to the choir loft to put on their robes and catch up on the latest news from their fellow choir members, while my brother and I cooled our heels until Sunday School started.

Through high school, Stan and I were in the same class, taught by the Harrison sisters, Marcie and Venita. Each week Stan used the extra time during this period to bedevil these kindly spinsters by writing fictitious Bible verses he spun out of thin air on the blackboard. They might say, "Unto Man nothing is possible, but unto God all things are possible. This does not include mothers, because they are not men," or "Verily I say unto you, that it is easier for a man to pass through

Christ stares down at the faithful from the expansive dome, his hand upraised, eternally blessing the congregation.

Stan used this period to bedevil the kindly spinsters by writing fictitious Bible verses he spun out of thin air on the blackboard.

SUMMER SUNDAY LUNCH

1 watermelon—chilled
Spicy salami—the kind you have to slice
    yourself
Thick slices of crusty bread: Greek, if you
    can find it, or substitute loaves of
    Italian or sweet French
Butter
Feta and Kasseri cheeses
Greek olives

1. Cut up the watermelon and place in serving bowl.
2. Slice salami, bread, and cheeses and place on plates.
3. Put the plates, bowl, as well as a plate of Greek olives and the butter on the table.
4. *Troyete!* Eat!
5. Follow the meal with fresh baked Greek pastries or cookies.

the eye of a needle than it is to get a surf board into the house past your mother." The two teachers let him start the class with a very brief lecture (more like a comedy routine) on the verse of the week, before they took over to discuss Miss Venita's favorite subject: the imminent Second Coming. She had the date of that cataclysmic event pegged for 1972.

After the services, my father hurried to C & K Imports, the Greek grocery store across the street from the cathedral to buy our weekly supply of Greek food. He would shop the shelves crowded with unusual and aromatic foods, including *feta* and *kasseri* cheeses, olives, Greek bread, oregano, as well as sweet delicacies and delights like *baklava* or pistachio *loukoumi*. He then rounded us up, and we headed home for a prolonged lunch. The four of us sat around the table, eating and talking about the week to come. During the summer we typically consumed the simple Summer Sunday Lunch, but to me it was a wonderful feast.

A FIG JAM

It's a warm, lazy late summer day in southern California in the early 1960s. I'm lounging in the back seat of my mother's white Chevy station wagon, while she drives my grandmother, *Yaya* Despina, across town to her home after her weekly visit to our family. I'm in my early teens, embarrassed by almost everything my family does; my *yaya* is in her seventies, beyond embarrassment. I'm startled from my state of reverie by my grandmother's cry, "Angela, *parakalo* (please), stop the car, *tora* (now)."

My mother stands on the brake, and I sit up to see *Yaya* quickly exit the car, slamming the door after her. To the side of us is a small white farmhouse dwarfed by the biggest fig tree I've ever seen, branches towering to the sky, full with heavy green bulbs of ripe fruit hanging below large, glossy leaves—more figs than anybody could eat in a lifetime. *Yaya* stands awestruck by its abundance for only a minute before she starts to pick the lower-hanging fruit. Lifting up the skirt of her house dress (exposing her sturdy, white legs to the oncoming traffic) she forms a basket in which to catch her stolen bounty.

"Mom," I say, "Stop her! She's stealing! We're going to get arrested."

"Relax. In the old country there's nothing wrong with folks just stopping by a fig tree on the road and picking the fruit for their own use," my mother explains. "*Yaya* doesn't think she's stealing, just sharing in Mother Nature's bounty."

"This isn't the old country," I mutter as I slouch down below the car window in dismay, not wanting to be taken as an accomplice to

Yaya starts to pick the lower-hanging fruit, lifting the skirt of her house dress (exposing her sturdy, white legs) to catch her stolen bounty.

If Yaya understood the English, she didn't understand that the owner would mind others taking from the tree what the owner's family could not possibly consume.

this very public breach of the law. I start counting the minutes, waiting for retribution to befall us.

As if cued by my thoughts, the owner of the fig tree stalks out of her house, calling to my grandmother to cease purloining her produce. I hold my breath. *Yaya* looks at her, smiles, and continues picking. She has conveniently decided that her English isn't good enough to understand the woman's irritated rant. My mother jumps out of the car, hurries to plant herself between the woman and my grandmother, and to explain the ethics and traditions of old Greece. The owner doesn't buy it any more than I did. My mother offers to pay for what *Yaya* has picked. The woman frowns. I'm paralyzed, fearing she will go further with her complaint, and I will witness my grandmother jailed.

Pursing her lips and shaking her head, the owner turns to my mother and says, "You don't have to pay me. Just take your mother-in-law away with the figs she's already filched, and don't come back again."

In Greek, my mother tells *Yaya* that the jig is up. With an inborn imperiousness, my grandmother picks a few more figs, and then gets into the car with her skirt full of fruit, nodding and smiling at the woman. If *Yaya* understood the English, she didn't understand the concept that the owner would mind others taking from the tree what the owner's family could not possibly consume. I start breathing again; my mother guns the car; and we make our getaway. When my mother drops *Yaya* off at the house she shared with Aunt Ginny and her family, she gives us a share of the take, gleefully carrying the rest into her kitchen.

What she did with all those figs I do not know. Twelve years later, after *Yaya* had died, my mother planted two fig trees in her backyard, two of the many prolific fruit trees in her small orchard. My mother and father were able to eat and give away all their prodigious harvests, especially since my mother was an avid preserver of food. From the need to preserve her sweet and tender figs she conjured up the following recipe, Angela's Fig Jam.

ANGELA'S FIG JAM

Yields 4–5 8-ounce Jars

4 cup fresh unpeeled figs, coarsely chopped
2 cups sugar
1 packet of "Sure Jell Pectin"
⅓ unpeeled orange, finely chopped
⅛ unpeeled lemon, finely chopped
½ cup toasted walnut meats, chopped
   (optional)

1. Toast the walnuts in a 350-degree oven for 8–10 minutes; chop.
2. Except for the optional walnuts, mix together all ingredients including any juices left on the chopping board surface.
3. Add barely enough water to start the fruit cooking, and then boil the mixture down until thick, cooking fast and stirring constantly (about 1 hour).
4. If desired, add chopped walnut meats just before pouring into sterilized jelly glasses. Seal with paraffin wax, or cap jars with canning seals and bands. Process in a water bath for 5 minutes.

NOTES

♥ Substitute 1 cup of the sugar with 1 cup honey.
■ To sterilize jars, put clean jars in a large, deep kettle. Cover with water to 1½ inches over the tops. Boil for 20 minutes. Leave jars in the water until ready to fill. Remove them using sterilized tongs.
■ With 8 cups figs use ¾ of an unpeeled orange, chopped and ¼ of an unpeeled lemon, chopped.

LOST RECIPES

Yaya gently taunted me as she popped the eyes into her mouth, claiming they were the tastiest part of all.

For many of the dishes my grandmothers and mother served, I simply can't locate the recipes. One example is pilaf, which was such a standard that nobody ever thought to write it down. I traveled to France to collect an interesting family recipe for pilaf from my French cousin (see page 167). Many other day-to-day dishes went undocumented as well. Some I can do without, like the fresh-water fish from Lake St. Claire that *Yaya* Despina used to bread and then fry with their heads and tails still attached. Their eyes stared out at those who ate them. *Yaya* gently taunted me as she popped the eyes into her mouth, claiming they were the tastiest part of all.

The recipe for *kolokithopita* is another prime example of a recipe MIA, a dessert that was part of the *Yaya* Wars on Thanksgiving. I have neither Despina's recipe for it, which called for homemade phyllo dough, nor Eleni's, which was the hands-down winner. *Yaya* Despina's Easter Bread is also lost to the ages.

In the case of *kolokithopitia*, I had to range beyond the Manolakas and Carlos families to recover this Greek dessert. Aunt Tootsie (nee Angela) is my Aunt Chubby's (nee Katherine) sister. Aunt Chubby was married to my father's brother, Lee. Even as the sister of an in-law we still considered Aunt Tootsie, her husband, Uncle Nick, and their four daughters family. Chubby and Tootsie's parents, Minnie and Steve Kirlakitsis also transcended the line between friendship and kinship. They were regulars at the family bridge parties, weddings, funerals, baptisms, and many holiday celebrations.

The Manolakas and Kirlakitsis families gather for Chubby and Lee's wedding, 1952

TOOTSIE'S KOLOKITHOPITA—PUMPKIN OR SQUASH PITA

Yields 20–25 pieces

Preheat oven 400 degrees

FILLING

2 lbs. banana squash or pumpkin
6 tbsp. butter
3½ cups scalded milk
3 tbsp. farina
¼ tsp. salt
1 cup sugar
8 eggs
2 tsp. vanilla
1 cup finely chopped walnuts

CRUST

1 cup finely chopped walnuts
Cinnamon, to taste
½ cup melted butter
1 lb. phyllo dough

SYRUP

2 cups sugar
1⅓ cup water
⅓ cup honey
1 cinnamon stick

1. Cut the peeled squash or pumpkin into cubes, and boil until soft. Put through a sieve or food processor.
2. Melt butter in a large pan, and stir in the squash/pumpkin mash.
3. In a separate pan, scald milk and add the farina. Mix and boil until the mixture thickens. Add the salt and sugar; boil approximately 15–20 minutes, stirring constantly, until its consistency is thick and custard-like.
4. Add the farina mixture into the squash/pumpkin mash. Blend well. Beat eggs until frothy, and beat into the custard/mash blend.
5. Add vanilla and 1 cup of ground walnuts to all. Cool.
6. (Refrigerate half of the phyllo sheets while using up the first half. The sheets that you are using should be kept in a dampened towel.) In a 9 x 13 inch baking pan, brush each phyllo sheet with melted butter and layer in this order:
- Sheets 1 & 2 of phyllo then sprinkle

Continued on next page

with ground nuts and cinnamon

- Sheets 3 & 4 of phyllo then sprinkle with ground nuts and cinnamon
- Sheets 5 & 6 of phyllo then sprinkle with ground nuts and cinnamon
- Sheets 7 & 8 of phyllo then pour and evenly spread the pumpkin filling
- Sheets 9 & 10 of phyllo then sprinkle with ground nuts and cinnamon
- Sheets 11 & 12 of phyllo then sprinkle with ground nuts and cinnamon
- Sheets 13 & 14 of phyllo then sprinkle with ground nuts and cinnamon
- Sheets 15 & 16 of phyllo then pour rest of melted butter on the top

7. With a sharp knife, cut the top pastry into 5 diagonal strips.

8. Bake in a preheated 400-degree oven for 15 minutes. Lower temperature to 350 degrees, and bake for about 1 hour or until golden.
9. While the custard is baking, combine the syrup ingredients in a saucepan. Bring to boil, and simmer for 15 minutes. Cool.
10. When the custard has finished baking, remove from oven and spoon COOL syrup over the hot kolokithopita. Do not cover the dessert or it will become soggy. Cool and cut into diamonds before serving.

OPTION

Use 2 small cans or 1 large canned pumpkin, instead of fresh cooked squash or pumpkin.

Party Girls in the early 1960s: Left to right: Chubby, friend, Mary Winders, Tootsie and Angela.

In the Greek culture, family can sometimes be loosely defined and include godchildren and their parents, and *sebetheda*. (This word was coined by the Greeks to describe the relationship between the husband's parents and the wife's parents. Therefore, Despina and Eleni were each other's *sebetheda*.) But I'm wandering.

Aunt Tootsie is a sweet, caring woman and a great cook in her own right. Try her *kolokithopita*; it is an exotic alternative to pumpkin pie on Thanksgiving. Another missing recipe was *bamias*, or braised okra, which *Yaya* Eleni made during the summers of my childhood. I grew

TOOTSIE'S BAMIAS—BRAISED OKRA

Yields 6 servings

1 onion, chopped
2 cloves garlic, minced
2 tbsp. olive oil
3–4 fresh tomatoes, chopped
Salt and pepper to taste
1 tsp. Italian seasonings
1½ tsp. dried oregano
2 tsp. dried basil
1 16-oz. package frozen cut okra
1 cup water, approximately

1. Sauté the onions and garlic in the olive oil until tender.

2. Add the tomatoes and seasonings, and simmer 15–20 minutes, stirring frequently.

3. Add the okra and water, and cook gently for 7–10 minutes, or until just tender. (Don't stir the okra too much or it will disintegrate.)

OPTION

Use fresh oregano and basil: 3 tbsp. chopped oregano and 6 tbsp. chopped basil

to love this dish with its tasty tomato sauce. Aunt Tootsie shared with me a more modern recipe of this dish. I have also included four more recipes from their branch of the "family," which she and Aunt Chubby were kind enough to share with me.

In another example of an old favorite lost, I could find no recipe in my mother's annuls for theples—a lacy dessert made by deep-frying a light batter that is either carefully strewn directly into a vat of heated oil per *Yaya* Despina's recipe or is formed by dipping a metal design

CHUBBY'S KARIDOPITA—WALNUT CAKE

Yields 16–20 servings

Preheat oven 350 degrees

SYRUP

2 cups water
1 tbsp. grated orange rind
2 cups sugar
½ tsp. orange flavoring

CAKE

2 cups "Bisquick"
½ cup sugar
1 cup chopped walnuts
1 cup milk
1 cup oil
4 beaten eggs
1 tbsp. grated orange rind
1½ tsp. baking powder
½ tsp. baking soda

½ tsp. cinnamon
½ tsp. nutmeg
1 tsp. cloves
1 tsp. orange flavoring

1. Combine the syrup ingredients into a saucepan, and bring to boil. Boil until the mixture is clear, approximately 30 minutes. Set out to cool while making the cake.
2. Add each of the cake ingredients to a bowl, mixing by hand after each addition until just blended.
3. Pour into a greased 9 x 13 inch cake pan, and cook in a preheated 350-degree oven for ½ hour.
4. Pour the cooled syrup over the hot cake. Let the cake cool before serving.

MINNIE'S SKORDALIA—GARLIC SAUCE WITH BLANCHED ALMONDS

Yields approximately 6½ cups

1 lb. blanched almonds
10–13 cloves of garlic, peeled
½ tsp. salt
10–12 ½-inch slices French or
    sourdough bread, crusts removed
1 cup olive oil
½ cup white vinegar (or juice of ½
    lemon and ¼ cup vinegar)
1 cup warm water
Salt to taste

1. In a food processor, grind blanched almonds to a ground meal. Remove from the processor.
2. Process the garlic cloves with ½ tsp. salt until the garlic is well crushed. Add in the ground nuts from step 1, and blend well.
3. Soak the bread in warm water, and squeeze the bread to remove the excess moisture.
4. Add the bread to the garlic mixture, and process until all are well mashed together.
5. Alternately add small amounts of the olive oil and vinegar, processing after each addition.
6. Add the warm water, and blend well. If thinner sauce is preferred, add a little more warm water. Salt to taste.

NOTES

- This sauce is used as an accompaniment to boiled beets, fried squash or eggplant, and fish or meat dishes.
- The sauce can be kept in the refrigerator for a couple of weeks.

DESPINA'S THEPLES—HONEY CURLS

DOUGH

7 eggs, well beaten
⅔ cup orange juice
½ tsp. baking soda
¼ cup whiskey
1¼ tsp. salt
5–7 cups flour (or more)
2–3 tbsp. vegetable oil

SYRUP

⅔ cup sugar
1⅓ cups water
1 cup honey
1 tsp. vanilla

1. Mix the orange juice with the baking soda, and then combine with eggs, whiskey, and salt. Mix thoroughly.
2. Sift in the flour, stirring it into the liquid mixture after each cup or less. Add the amount of flour until it resembles raw pie crust (i.e., a heavy dough that is still a little crumbly).
3. Add the oil, and knead into the dough until it doesn't stick to your hands.
4. Divide the dough into potato-sized balls, and roll each until paper-thin. Cut the thin dough into 1½–2 inch strips.
5. Using forks, drop the dough into oil brought to a slow boil over medium heat. As it cooks, shape it into a knot with the forks. After it cooks to a light golden color, remove from the oil and lay on a paper towel to cool.
6. Make syrup by combine sugar and water in a saucepan; bring to boil. Simmer over low heat until syrupy (about 15 minutes).
7. Add honey and vanilla, and simmer 5 minutes longer.
8. Dribble honey syrup over the fried dough, and sprinkle with finely chopped nuts.

MINNIE'S COPENHEIM

Yields 24–30 pieces

Preheat oven 400 degrees

SYRUP

4 cups sugar
1 lemon, juiced and then sliced
3 cups water

CUSTARD

12 eggs, separated
1 cup sugar
1 lb. almonds with skins, coarsely ground
1 tsp. vanilla
1 tsp. cinnamon

CRUST

1 lb. phyllo
¾ lb. unsalted butter

1. Make the syrup first by combining the three ingredients and bring to a boil. Simmer over medium heat about 40–45 minutes, until the liquid becomes syrupy. Cool completely.

Copenheim: nut filled and juicy with syrup

2. Line a 10 x 16 inch pan with 10–12 phyllo sheets, buttering each sheet as you layer them into the pan. Let any extra length or width of pastry hang over the rim of the pan.
3. Beat eggs yolks and then add sugar, beating the mixture until light and fluffy.
4. Beat the egg whites separately until they form stiff peaks.

Continued on next page

5. Slowly fold in almonds, cinnamon, and vanilla into the egg yolks. Than fold in egg whites.

6. Pour the egg mixture over the phyllo sheets in the pan. Then overlap the extra phyllo hanging over the rim onto the top of the egg mixture.

7. Layer the rest of the phyllo sheets on top of the mixture, brushing butter between each sheet. With a sharp knife, score through the top layers of phyllo where you will cut the pieces.

8. Bake at 400 degrees for 10 minutes. Then lower the oven temperature to 375 degrees and bake for 35–40 minutes or until golden brown.

9. When you remove the custard from the oven, slowly pour the cold syrup over the hot cake.

into the batter and then plunging the coated design into the hot pot per *Yaya* Eleni's method. The resulting crisp is then coated with honey syrup, chopped nuts, and cinnamon. I was sad to think the recipe had been lost. It wasn't until I recently talked to Aunt Betty, Uncle George Manolakas' wife, about the loss that she pawed through her stack of old recipes and unearthed it. While Eleni's is still missing, Despina's is provided on page 124.

GREEK SALAD

A fresh, piquant offering, the Greek salad makes an excellent side dish or meal.

In America, one of the better-known authentic Greek dishes is Greek salad. A fresh, piquant offering, the Greek salad makes an excellent side dish or a meal in itself. My mother served us this salad at least four times a week. She may have varied the vegetables, depending on the season and what she had on hand, but she always dressed it in the same way, and we never tired of it. On the contrary, her dressing was so tasty that Fred, my first husband, swore that one of the reasons he married me was because he liked it so much. It is very easy to make,

ANGELA'S GREEK SALAD

TRADITIONAL INGREDIENTS

A variety of greens, chopped or torn into
  bite sized pieces (see options)
Wedges of tomato
Slices of cucumber
Thin slices of yellow or red onions
Feta cheese, chunked or crumbled
Kalamata olives
Garlic or garlic granules
Salt, pepper, and oregano

ADDITIONAL INGREDIENTS

Chopped green and red pepper
Chopped green onions (my mother's
  choice of onion)
Sliced radishes
Sliced carrots
Chopped fresh parsley
Chunked avocado

To make the salad dressing the
traditional way, rub a large wooden salad
bowl with garlic. Or you can sprinkle the
vegetables with garlic granules.

1. Prepare vegetables as described above
   and place in the salad bowl.
2. Sprinkle with salt, pepper, and oregano.
   If I have them on hand, I will add
   chopped fresh basil or mint.
3. Douse the vegetables with olive oil and
   apple cider or wine vinegar (more olive
   oil than vinegar).

OPTIONS

- Dressing proportions, if "dousing" is too
  cavalier for your comfort: 1 part vinegar
  to 2 parts olive oil.
- Lemon juice can be used instead of
  vinegar.
- Typically, in the United States lettuce
  means iceberg, but romaine and other
  lettuces, beet greens, spinach, and
  dandelion greens may also be added.

and after a couple of tries you will learn to proportion the ingredients to suit your taste.

FOUR BEAN SALAD

Like many of us, my mother sometimes got stuck in a recipe rut. If the dish were something she could keep refrigerated for a week or store frozen, it would most likely be added to her list of regulars. Some, like her Spanish Sandwiches, we feared seeing her pull out of the freezer, thaw, and toast in the oven for lunch. But her four bean salad was so good that my children and I wolfed it down every time she put it on the table. She served it constantly the last 20 years of her life, making it in large quantities and leaving it in the refrigerator to serve up throughout the week. Because the salad lasted well and provided a piquant side dish to both lunches and dinners, it became a staple on her party menus, as well as at picnics and potluck offerings. She discovered the basic recipe at a potluck where she worked, and making some characteristic changes to the dressing and adding the Greek touch of garbanzo beans, she adapted it to be one of her signature Greek-inspired American dishes.

RICE PUDDING

For most of her life my mother was an adventurous cook, trying new recipes and revising even more, but as she grew older her cooking, while still fabulous, settled into old standards. We counted on a steady supply of Greek *koulourakia*, fresh salads, and pastitsio. And Charlie and Sally, my children and her grandchildren, could rely on their Yaya greeting them at the door with a bowl of rice pudding, even when they grew into their twenties.

Why she decided on this dessert as the staple of all their visits is a mystery. Maybe she thought that with its ingredients of eggs and milk,

We depended on those dishes of cool pudding to soothe our throats and tummies after our long ride.

ANGELA'S FOUR BEAN SALAD

Servings: 12–16

1 lb. can of cut green beans, drained
1 lb. can kidney beans, drained and rinsed
1 lb. can of cut wax beans, drained
1 lb. can of garbanzo beans, drained and
    rinsed
⅔ cup chopped green and/or red
    peppers
⅔ cup onions, chopped

DRESSING

⅔ cup vinegar
⅓ cup vegetable oil
½ cup sugar
1 tsp. salt
¼ tsp. pepper

1. Mix the beans together in a large
   bowl.
2. Add the peppers and onions into the
   mix.
3. Mix all the dressing ingredients
   together.
4. Pour the dressing onto vegetable mix.
   Toss and chill for at least an hour
   before serving.

Four Bean Salad: Quick, easy, and delicious

OPTIONS

♥ As time passed my mother used little to
  no sugar in the recipe. I have substituted
  ¼ cup agave syrup for the sugar, which
  makes a delicious and healthier dressing.
♥ My mother advised using less than the
  ⅓ cup oil to cut down on the amount
  of fat.

ANGELA'S RICE PUDDING

Yields 6 servings

4 cups milk
½ cup sugar (or less)
½ cup long grain white rice
½ cup water
½ cup raisins
Dash salt
2 eggs, beaten
1 tsp. vanilla
Cinnamon

1. Combine milk, sugar, rice, raisins, water, and salt in a heavy 4 qt. saucepan.
2. Slowly bring to a boil, stirring constantly. Reduce heat and simmer, uncovered. Stir frequently for 35 to 45 minutes, until rice is tender and the mixture has a slightly thickened consistency.
3. Remove from heat. Slowly stir in the eggs, beating constantly to keep the eggs from congealing while the heated mixture cooks them. Then stir in the vanilla.
4. Pour the pudding into a 1½ qt. baking dish. Sprinkle the top with cinnamon. Cool.

OPTION

♥ Replace the sugar with ¼–⅓ cup agave nectar.

it was a healthy way to please their penchant for sweets. Or maybe my Dad loved it, so she satisfied both *Papou* and the grandchildren with this offering. Regardless, for the last ten years of her life, she must have made gallons of the stuff.

The funny thing was, as the years went on, we came to depend on that large casserole dish full of pudding to be waiting for us when we came to visit. Its cool, creamy consistency and gentle sweetness soothed our throats and tummies after our long ride from San Diego to my parents' Whittier home. We would wolf down that first serving and follow-up with one bowl a day each until the pan was scraped clean.

As the years passed my mother started to fiddle with the recipe. When my father became diabetic, she learned to make it with artificial sweetener. When he had to watch his cholesterol, she substituted non-fat milk. Each rendition was slightly different from the traditional recipe, but each was equally delicious. The following recipe is her old standard. She did not codify any of her later substitutions and changes.

ROAST LEG OF LAMB

The Greeks love their lamb. It is the primary food at any feast, as well as a common repast throughout the year. My husband Steven and I laughed in shocked recognition when Aunt Voula in *My Big, Fat Greek Wedding* told Toula and Ian (the bride and her prospective, vegetarian bridegroom) that since he ate no meat, she would cook lamb when they came to dinner. My mother said virtually the same thing to my vegetarian husband when she first met him. To the Greeks, not eating lamb is inconceivable, rising above any one category of food. It is not meat; it is lamb.

One of the best known of Greek dishes, its distinctive preparation imparts a unique taste. The Greeks choose succulent young lambs, eschewing mutton because of its strong, almost gamey taste. After they suffuse the meat with garlic and herbs, they roast it until it is well done.

Having been raised on lamb roasted after the Greek fashion, I was surprised when I was first served American leg of lamb by my first mother-in-law, Dorothy. My slice was pink and chewy, and except for the mint jelly that was served with it, the meat was almost tasteless. I was used to my roast being cooked well done, yet still tender and juicy. The garlic, oregano, and lemon juice enhanced the distinctive taste of

To the Greeks, not eating lamb is inconceivable, rising above any one category of food. It is not meat; it is lamb.

ANGELA'S ROAST LEG OF LAMB—ARNI PSITO

Yields 8 servings

Preheat oven to 450 degrees

1 leg of lamb
4–6 garlic cloves
2 tbsp. melted butter
Salt and pepper
Dried oregano
Juice of 1 lemon
Water

1. Wash the leg of lamb and with a sharp pointed knife make deep slits in top and sides of the leg.
2. Slice garlic cloves into 2 or 3 slices (10–12 pieces of garlic), and push each 1 of the slices deeply into each of the slits you have made.
3. Place the leg into a roasting pan fat side up, brush with melted butter, and season with salt, pepper, and oregano. Squeeze the juice of 1 lemon over the lamb.
4. Roast the leg for 30 minutes in the 450-degree oven. Then lower the heat to 350 degrees and add about a cup or so of water. Roast the leg for 2–3 more hours, depending on the size of the roast. Add more water to the pan if needed.

OPTIONS

- Add 8–10 potatoes, peeled and quartered, to the roasting pan about 1½ hours before the roast is done. Prepare the potatoes beforehand by rubbing the pieces with a small amount of tomato paste (optional) and sprinkling with salt, pepper, garlic granules, and oregano. Turn and baste the potatoes occasionally. If the potatoes aren't brown when the leg is done, remove the leg, increase the oven temperature to 425 degrees, and brown the potatoes 20 minutes longer.
- Serve the leg of lamb with a rice pilaf (see page 167).
- Traditionally, especially if you are serving the lamb with orzo or pilaf, serve plain yogurt as a side dish with the dinner. Its piquant taste nicely sets off the taste of the rich, sweet lamb.

ANGELA'S LAMB AND ORZO ROASTED IN THE PAN

Yields 6–8 servings

Lamb leg prepared for roasting (see
    previous recipe)
3 cups orzo
4 cups hot water
Salt, pepper, and garlic powder to taste

1. Roast leg of lamb in the oven for 2½
   hours at 350 degrees.
2. Raise the oven temperature to 375,
   and add the hot water.
3. Stir in the orzo, and sprinkle it with
   salt, pepper, and garlic powder.
4. Bake 30–40 minutes, stirring
   occasionally, until pasta is al dente.
5. Serve immediately, sprinkled with
   grated mizithra, Parmesan, or Romano
   cheese.

OPTION

Add 15-oz. can chopped stewed tomatoes
when you add the hot water. Reduce
amount of water to 2¾ cups.

the meat. My meal of lamb was always served with an accompaniment
of tangy yogurt.

    I have learned to appreciate both tastes; however, I still prefer the
tender aromatic slices of the Greek roast, served with roasted potatoes,
orzo, or rice pilaf cooked in the meat's drippings.

MY BROTHER AND SISTER-IN-LAW

I was blessed with one sibling, my brother Stanton (a.k.a. Stamatios,
Stan, Stantoint, Stantonstupeytine, and Capitan Stamati), who

Close in age, we also created our own worldview, which drove our parents nuts. We liked it that way.

preceded me into this world by 19 months. We were not only close in age, we also created our own worldview, which on most occasions drove our parents nuts. We liked it that way.

We shared most of our playmates, either concocting elaborate stories or war to act out or making up games. We played our favorite game with the Stevens' girls who lived next door to our cottage, which happened to be situated by railroad tracks. There was only one rule to that game: when trains traveled by our houses ten to fifteen times a day, we had to climb up on something and stay there until the last car passed. If we failed to do so, we would be "run over." Fast moving passenger trains would sneak up on us, causing us to scurry to a safe perch. Or a long freight train would lumber by, marooning us until the caboose disappeared around the bend. If we were swimming in the lake, we floated while the train passed, and if we were playing in our large front yard, we ran to the stones and logs that lined the road and quickly climbed onto them. Our parents had to wait for us to do their bidding until we climbed off our safe perches and resumed our activities. If perchance we were caught on the ground and we were "run over," we would mope, depressed, for the rest of the day.

Connie and Angie at their 50th Wedding Anniversary celebration, 1989

My brother was also my most avid food critic, especially in his wise-cracking teen-age years. He would sit in exaggerated judgment of my cakes: "I almost broke my fork eating this"; my cookies: "You burnt this tray"; and my entrees: "I like hamburgers and French fries better." The nicest things he ever voiced were grunts and snarfing sounds, as he gobbled up something he liked. But then, what are older brothers for?

POULA'S RAVANI

Yields 12–16 pieces

Preheat oven 350 degrees

CAKE

½ lb. softened butter
1 cup sugar
5 eggs
2½ cups self-rising flour (sifted)
1 tsp. vanilla extract

SYRUP

1 cup sugar
1½ cup water
1 tbsp. lemon juice
2 tbsp. honey

1. Cream butter and sugar until pale and fluffy.
2. Add eggs, one at a time, beating after each addition.
3. Fold in sifted flour. Then add the vanilla extract. Batter should be thick and smooth.
4. Grease and flour a 9 x 13 inch pan. Distribute batter across the pan and spread until smooth and even.
5. Bake in a 350-degree oven for 25–35 minutes, until done. Test by inserting a toothpick in center of the cake. It should come out clean.
6. While the cake is baking, combine the syrup ingredients into a saucepan. Bring the liquid to a boil, and stir while simmering over a low heat for twenty minutes.
7. After the cake is cool, cut into pieces, and pour the syrup all over the top of the cake. Let it sit for an hour, to allow the syrup to soak into the cake.

He bartered her recipes, "If you go out with me, I'll give you my mother's secret cookie recipe."

He also was a fan of my mother's cooking. He showed his appreciation for her recipes by bartering them for dates and marriage proposals, as in, "If you go out with me, I'll give you my mother's secret cookie recipe." Mom's salad dressing recipe was also in his arsenal of enticements.

I'm not sure that his wife Barbara married him for either recipe, but he was able to do something nobody else did from our large group of cousins. He married a Greek girl. This was a cause of great celebration for the home team and its two coaches (my grandmothers) who constantly harangued us during our formative years to "marry a good Greek [boy or girl]."

In 1971, we all trekked to Cleveland, Ohio, Barbara's hometown, to their big Greek wedding. My son, Charlie, was three weeks old at the time. Pictures of Stan and Barbara's wedding show my first husband, Fred, holding tiny Charlie in a green baby seat, with a big congratulatory cigar hanging from proud papa's mouth. On the other side of the generational divide, my big, fat Greek *Yaya* Despina was 81 years old, which did not stop her from getting up in her fancy dress, hat, and three-inch stacked heels to dance in the Greek line dances. *Opa!*

Stan and Barb settled in Los Angeles, where they are still plugged into the Greek community. Barbara has always been a great Greek hostess, sharing her family's versions of Greek recipes. She has also been a great guest, a tireless worker when my mother's banquets were served and clean-up help was needed. This cookbook wouldn't be complete without recipes from Barbara Soldathos Manolakas. Both are cake recipes, the first from her girlfriend's mother, *Thea* Poula, and the second from her Auntie Maritza.

MARITZA'S KARIDOPITA—NUT CAKE

Yields 18–24 pieces

Preheat oven to 350 degrees

¼ lb. butter
½ cup sugar
6 eggs
¼ cup milk
5 tsp. baking powder
I tsp. cinnamon
I cup finely ground zwieback or wheat
    rusks
I cup flour
2 cups chopped walnuts

SYRUP

2¾ cups water
1¾ cups sugar
I tbsp. honey
A few drops lemon juice

Karidopita: A tasty way to get your
Omega-3 oil

1. Beat butter and sugar together.
2. Add eggs one at a time. Then add milk.
3. In a clean bowl mix cinnamon and zwieback, and add to the above mixture.
4. In a clean bowl mix baking powder with flour, and add to rest of the mixture.
5. Fold in nuts.
6. Spread the batter into the greased 9 x 13 inch cake pan, and bake for 30 minutes.
7. While baking, prepare the syrup by mixing all ingredients in a saucepan. Bring it to a boil, and simmer for 20–30 minutes, stirring occasionally.
8. Let the cake cool, and cut it into serving pieces. With the cake still in the pan, pour warm syrup over the entire cake. Let it stand for a while, until the cake and syrup have totally cooled.

My Greek Kitchen

My mother didn't make the same mistake as her mother did of not teaching her daughter to cook. She started me very early, at age seven. The first recipe she asked me to assist her with was making *koulourakia*—Greek cookies. I was given the task of cracking the eggs into the dough while her old Mixmaster beaters mixed in all the ingredients. Standing on my step stool to reach the counter, I did well with the first two eggs. Alas, with the third I dropped an eggshell into the batter. In seconds, the beaters ground the shell into many tiny pieces that my mother and I then tried to pick out. The cookies were good if you didn't mind crunching through the remaining eggshells. Based on the number of my brother's complaints, he minded a lot. But I fared much better with my next venture and those thereafter.

When I was in eighth grade I cooked my first full meal as a homework assignment for Home Economics class. I was directed by my teacher to schedule all my activities and then follow the schedule to make the dinner by a pre-appointed time. I used the example in the textbook, giving myself 10 minutes for this, 15 for that. My mother read through my plan and expressed some doubts over it. She thought I should allow more time. In my characteristic stubbornness and independence, I ignored her. What did Mom know anyway? Could her years of cooking experi-

Elaine, Sally, and Charles at their Coronado, CA home, 1981

ELENI'S KOULOURAKIA

Yields 6–8 dozen cookies for each recipe

Preheat oven for both recipes 350 degrees

1 lb. butter
1½ cup sugar
3 eggs, beaten
2 cups milk
2 tsp. vanilla, or ¼ cup ouzo or whiskey
10–12 cups flour
2 tbsp. + 1 tsp. baking powder
1 egg yolk
Sesame seeds

1. Cream butter until fluffy, and then gradually beat in the sugar.
2. Beat 3 eggs until light, then add to butter mixture; beat thoroughly. Beat in milk and then the vanilla, or ouzo or whiskey.
3. Mix together the first 4 cups of flour with the baking powder, and slowly fold into the butter and egg mixture. Continue adding the flour until the dough is smooth and firm enough to be rolled into different shapes. Chill.
4. Roll into various lengths, about ½ inch in diameter, and then form into different koulourakia shapes, e.g. 3 inch lengths for circles and spirals; 6 inch lengths doubled lengthwise or doubled lengthwise and twisted into a simple braid. (Use about 2–3 tbsp. of dough to form each of the shapes.)
5. Place shapes on cookie sheets. Brush with beaten egg yolk mixed with about a tsp. of water and sprinkle with sesame seeds.
6. Bake in preheated oven at 350 degrees for 30–35 minutes or until lightly browned on top.

NOTE

Yield depends on the cookie sizes and shapes you make. If you make half the recipe add 1 egg and 1 egg white, reserving the yolk for the egg wash.

ence measure up to the authority of an impersonal textbook? Not to this twelve-year-old.

So I started. I felt I was rushing around like a madwoman, and my mother's observations confirmed it. She said watching me reminded her of a movie running double-time or Lucy and Ethel at the candy factory. As I made my meatloaf, twice-baked potatoes, spinach, salad, and lemon meringue pie, I spilled flour, bumped around the kitchen, and horror of horrors, dropped a fleck of egg yolk into the meringue. (Egg failures seemed to be my cooking instruction nemesis.) That really stalled me. From that experience I learned it only takes a fleck of yolk to stop the foaming action of egg whites. I beat and beat and beat those whites, only to produce a sickly, liquidity blanket of white to cover my perfect lemon custard. I baked it anyway, but I missed the mark of creating a light, fluffy meringue.

I was spared the pain of my brother's taunting, since he and my father were out on an overnight event. And my mother assured me that everything I had made was tasty, even the pie. We had a hearty laugh at dinner about my manic preparations, and I learned a lot from the exercise—which is, after all, the point of homework assignments.

For three weeks during the summer before my junior year in high school, I took over cooking dinner for the family. I was a novice chef by then. First, I would read through cookbooks and magazines to select my recipes. Next I would make out my menus and shopping lists for my father to use when he bought the groceries. Each morning I would make the dessert and then proceed leisurely through the afternoon making delectable choices to delight my family's palate. We all loved that brief period, and I came into my own as a cook.

As I grew up I expanded my repertoire, always treasuring most the Greek recipes that had been passed down to me. Armed with my experience and those recipes, by the time I was married I was ready for all the entertaining and bake sales required of me as a naval officer's wife.

I spilled flour, bumped around the kitchen, and horror of horrors, dropped a fleck of egg yolk into the meringue.

With Greek recipes this creep accelerates to a trot due to the different geographical versions of the same dish.

RECIPE CREEP

Have you noticed that in this book there are several recipes for the same offering, each one a little different from the others? I've already shared two *Spanakopita* recipes, three *koulourakia* recipes, and a version of *Galatoboureko*. I call this phenomenon recipe creep. It's what happens when people use traditional recipes and add their personal twist. With Greek recipes this creep accelerates to a trot due to the different geographical versions of the same dish. An example: my Cretan family members used cinnamon in their meat dishes; the Chioti faction did not.

Purchase a copy of a Greek cookbook published by any Greek church's women's society to find further confirmation of this phenomenon. In one book I own, an old standard originally published in 1961, there are two recipes of similar *keftaides* (cocktail meatballs), four recipes for *tiropites* (cheese puffs), and six recipes for roast leg of lamb.

My family recipes also span over a century—with many changes in available and even desirable ingredients. So along with the original recipes I have added to recipe creep by recommending healthy options based on the imperatives of modern health science. Believe me, no Greek ever used buffalo meat in their traditional dishes until, maybe, this century.

The two recipes in this section are great examples of recipe creep. Here I have provided Yaya Eleni's original version of a Greek dessert, *Galatoboureko*, a luscious combination of custard and phyllo saturated with sweet syrup. I have also provided my mother's evolution of the dish. The latest rendition of the family *Galatoboureko* recipe is Aunt Kathryn's, listed on page 93. Each is different, and each is wonderful.

ELENI'S GALATOBOUREKO

Serves 24

Preheat oven 350 degrees

SYRUP

2½ cups water
2½ cups sugar
Juice of ½ lemon
1 cinnamon stick

CUSTARD

1 qt. milk
1⅓ cup sugar
6 oz. cornstarch
3 egg yolks
1 whole egg
1 tsp. vanilla
½ lb. butter, melted
1 lb. phyllo dough

1. First, combine syrup ingredients in a pan and bring to boil. Simmer for 15 minutes. Cool completely while you prepare the pastry.
2. Mix milk and sugar together in a pan and bring to boil over medium heat, stirring constantly.
3. Beat the egg yolks and egg together with the cornstarch. Slowly add 1 cup of the milk and sugar mixture to the eggs, beating constantly. Then slowly add the hot egg mixture into the rest of the milk and sugar mixture, again stirring constantly.
4. Add vanilla and cool slightly.
5. Place half of the sheets of phyllo in a well-buttered 9 x 13 inch pan, brushing each sheet generously with melted butter before putting them into the pan. (Refrigerate half of the sheets while using up the first half. The sheets that you are using should be kept in a dampened towel.)
6. Pour the cream mixture into the pan, and top with the remaining phyllo, once again brushing each piece generously with melted butter.
7. With a sharp knife, cut the top pastry into 4 or 5 strips.
8. Bake in a preheated 350-degree oven for 45 minutes or until lightly browned.
9. When the custard has finished baking, remove from the oven, and pour the COOL syrup over the hot galatoboureko. Cool and cut into squares before serving. Do not cover the pan, or it will make the dessert soggy.

ANGELA'S GALATOBOUREKO

Serves 24

Preheat oven 375 degrees

SYRUP

2½ cups boiling
  water
3½ cups sugar
1 tsp. lemon juice
1 cinnamon stick
  (optional)

CUSTARD

1½ quarts warm
  milk
8 egg yolks
1½ cup sugar
6 tbsp. cornstarch
1 tbsp. vanilla
1 cup heavy cream
½ lb. butter, melted
1 lb. phyllo dough

1. First, combine syrup ingredients in a pan and bring to boil. Simmer for 15 minutes. Cool completely while you prepare the pastry.
2. Heat the milk in a saucepan until warm.
3. Beat egg yolks and sugar until mixture is thick and pale in color.
4. Slowly add 1 cup of milk alternately with cornstarch to the egg and sugar mixture, beating constantly. Then slowly add the hot egg and sugar mixture into the rest of the milk, again beating constantly.
5. Cook over low heat, stirring constantly, until mixture almost reaches a boil.
6. Remove from heat, and add vanilla and cream. Cool slightly.
7. Place half of the sheets of phyllo in a well-buttered 9 x 13 inch pan, brushing each sheet generously with melted butter before putting them in the pan. (Refrigerate half of the sheets while using up the first half. The sheets that you are using should be kept in a dampened towel.)
8. Pour the cream mixture into the pan, and top with the remaining phyllo, once again brushing each piece generously with melted butter.
9. With a sharp knife, cut top pastry into 4 or 5 strips.
10. Bake in a preheated 375-degree oven for 45 or 50 minutes or until lightly browned.
11. When the custard has finished baking, remove from the oven, and pour the COOL syrup over the hot galatoboureko. Cool and cut into squares before serving. Do not cover the pan, or it will make the dessert soggy.

YANKEE POT ROAST

When I first married, at the unbelievably young age of twenty, I moved with my naval aviator husband, Fred Hawes, from urban Los Angeles to rural, southern Pensacola, Florida. To help me feel at home I took with me a carton of cookbooks and recipe cards from my mother's Greek kitchen.

In the second year of our southern adventure I discovered I was missing one important recipe—my mother's tasty Greek beef stew. It was a rich and hardy dish, with a spicy tomato sauce and big chunks of meat—perfect for the cold, rainy winter days in Pensacola. I phoned her to request it.

"Greek beef stew?" she responded. "I don't have a Greek stew recipe. What are you talking about?"

"You know," I said. "The one with the tomato sauce with cinnamon, the one you serve with peas and mashed potatoes."

"Oh, you mean my Yankee Pot Roast."

Yankee Pot Roast! No Yankee had ever put cinnamon in her pot roast; nor would any Rebel I had met here in the South. I guessed my mother had found the recipe in a magazine and added her personal touch to it—the Greek touch of olive oil, garlic, and cinnamon. Not all Greeks grace their meat dishes with cinnamon, nor is it to everybody's taste. In fact, it constituted a large part of the great Carlos-Manolakas food divide. I stand on the Carlos side of that divide. To me cinnamon imparts mystery and a delicate sweetness to any meat, sauce, or casserole. And it makes this "Yankee" pot roast uniquely delicious.

Yankee Pot Roast! No Yankee had ever put cinnamon in her pot roast; nor would any Rebel I had met here in the South.

ANGELA'S YANKEE POT ROAST

Yields 4 servings

1 lb. round steak, cubed
1 onion, chopped
3 cloves garlic, minced
3 tbsp. olive oil
6-oz. can tomato paste
1 cup water
8-oz. can of tomato sauce
1 bay leaf
1 tsp. cinnamon
Salt and pepper to taste
1 cup frozen peas
¾ cup sliced carrots

1. Cut round steak into 1-inch chunks, and brown with chopped onion in olive oil.

2. In the last few minutes of browning add 3 minced cloves of garlic.
3. Add tomato paste, water, tomato sauce, and spices. Stir into a smooth sauce.
4. Add frozen peas and carrots, and simmer for one hour.
5. Serve with mashed potatoes or spaghetti.

OPTIONS

♥ For an extremely lean, tender, and tasty meat, substitute buffalo steak for beef.
■ If you like, you can add more vegetables. I have made this stew adding zucchini, broccoli, and green beans along with the peas and carrots.

FORAGING FOR FOOD

The old country Greeks found many of their cooking ingredients growing in the wild. They foraged for basil, oregano, and mint. They harvested the honey of local beehives, and picked the grape leaves

Despina's Dolmadakia me Avgolemono
—Stuffed Grape Leaves with Egg/Lemon Sauce

Yields approximately 75 pieces

3 lb. ground beef
½ cup chopped onions
½ cup chopped celery
½ cup chopped parsley
2 tbsp. butter
Salt and pepper to taste
½ cup rice
1 egg, beaten
¼ cup olive oil
½ cup water
1 cup lemon juice
Jars of grape leaves equal to 1½ lbs.
Water and butter

Grape leaves stuffed with meat and rice, rinsed with an egg-lemon sauce

1. Sauté onions, celery, and parsley in butter until soft.
2. Add in ground meat and brown.
3. Add the rest of the ingredients, except the grape leaves, and mix well.
4. Set aside.
5. Drain brine from a jar of pickled grape leaves; remove leaves from the jar. Separate and wash them with clear water to remove all traces of the brine.
6. Put a heaping tbsp. of meat and rice mixture in the center of each leaf and roll tightly, by first folding the top of the leaf over the meat, folding the edges tightly inward, and then rolling from the top down toward the bottom point of the leaf.
7. Cover bottom of a greased Dutch oven or kettle with torn leaves. Arrange rolls on top of the leaves in layers.

Continued on next page

8. Add enough water to cover rolls, and dot with butter.
9. Cover the rolls with a heavy plate to keep them from opening as the rice cooks. Cover the pot, and steam over low heat on top of the stove for 1 to 1½ hours. There should be some liquid left in the pot for sauce. (If dry when the cooking time is up, then add water and simmer for a few minutes longer.

Egg/Lemon Sauce

3 eggs
Juice of 1 lemon

1. Separate eggs. Beat whites until firm peaks form. Fold in yolks.
2. Add lemon juice.
3. Slowly add the hot liquid from the pot into the egg mixture, beating constantly to avoid curdling the eggs.

4. When the egg mixture is very warm and well beaten, pour it over the dolmadakia.
5. Serve at once. If it is necessary to reheat, leave uncovered, and warm slowly to avoid having the egg sauce curdle.

Options

♥ Substitute ground buffalo for the ground beef for a leaner version.
■ Add lamb as part or all of the 3 lbs. of ground meat.
■ Use 2 tbsp. tomato juice or ketchup instead of the 1 cup lemon juice.
■ If you use fresh grape leaves, gather them when they are young and tender, the wild variety preferably. Cut off the stems, and wash the leaves thoroughly. Blanch them briefly in hot water before rolling the *dolmadakia*.

from their neighbors' in which they wrapped their food. Dandelions, which we consider weeds, were trimmed from the fields and served as vegetable greens and salads. The enterprising Greeks even used pine sap for flavoring and to make wine and liquor.

Both of my grandmothers passed on to me this passion for plucking from the wilds the goodness of Mother Earth for their tables. It satisfies me to find something edible and healthy growing of its own

ELAINE'S DANDELION GREENS

Yields 2 cups of fresh greens yield 1 serving

Fresh picked, young dandelion greens (2–4 cups)
Water and/or olive oil
White wine, balsamic vinegar, or lemon juice

1. Although you can buy dandelion greens in some health food stores, I prefer to pick my plants from my lawn. They are best picked early in the spring, before the hot sun makes them bitter. You can select individual leaves or whole crowns. Cut off the roots and wash the leaves thoroughly.

2. There are three main ways to cook the leaves: steaming, boiling, and sautéing in oil. Steamed and boiled dandelions are the most tender.

- Steaming: Place in vegetable steamer and cook for 5 or more minutes, until tender.
- Boiling: Add leaves to a small amount of boiling water. Cook for 5 minutes or more, until tender. Serve the remaining juice with the leaves.
- Sautéing: In a deep pot, sauté 2 cloves of garlic, minced, and a scant $\frac{1}{4}$ cup finely chopped onions in 1 tbsp. olive oil, until tender. Add 4 cups of leaves, and sauté until wilted. (Serves 2.)

3. Dress the cooked vegetables with olive oil and white wine vinegar, balsamic vinegar, or lemon juice. I typically use only olive oil and lemon juice, the traditional Greek dressing.

volition in my back yard. I harvest it, fresh off the vine or stalk, for the bubbling pot.

In the summer at our cottage, my *Yaya* Despina had a ready supply of grape leaves and mint. We would spy her early in the morning, gathering the grape leaves from vines that grew wild on our next-door-neighbor's fence, and would wrap the *dolmadakia* she made for dinner that evening. She would pick the leaves that were both large and tender, catching them in her apron. After washing and briefly blanching them, she would fill them with a seasoned ground meat and rice filling and roll them into neat little flavor packets. The hearty, rich meat flavor of this dish is balanced by the piquant grape leaves and tangy egg-lemon sauce. If you have no grapevines close to your house to forage, you can buy jars of grape leaves pickled in brine.

Dandelion greens are another source of food that many modern cooks overlook, thinking of them as a weed. In the spring in Detroit, our lawn grew a mass of dandelions. My mother and I would dig them out with butter knives from the front yard. Our lawn would look better for the effort, and we would have our vegetable for dinner that evening.

She shared a memory with me that on the weekends when she was small, her family would take the streetcar out of the city to a park at the end of the line. The family included my mother's aunt and her many children. All of them would picnic and then harvest the greens from the surrounding grass. They would ride the streetcar home with greens for their supper.

Because the foraging gene lives on in me, today Steven and I let volunteer blackberry bushes grow in our backyard that provide berries for our morning cereal. I have a patch of mint, which escaped through the bottom of the pot I planted it in and had once taken over a large area of our yard. I can pluck it to season my casseroles, to brighten up my summer drinks, or I can just chew it to refresh my breath. I have planted grapes—not for the fruit, but to have a ready supply of fresh grape leaves, which can't be bought at the store. And I harvest the dandelions in the spring, before they get bitter, to sauté and eat, doused with olive oil and lemon juice.

COMMUNAL COOKING: A WORD OF ADVICE

After making 150 rolls of stuffed grape leaves or a complicated phyllo dish, I have decided that most Greek recipes must have been developed in a communal environment. I imagine the women of the family or the village gathering in the largest kitchen to help each other prepare for the next important feast day. "Many hands make light work," the proverb says, and the women would laugh and gossip as they made the delicious traditional recipes.

Initially, I came close to that experience when my mother taught me how to make Greek food. We would labor in her kitchen, calling my father in to help when it was time for all the rolling and shaping that the recipe required. I treasure the memory of our family closeness at those times.

However, it was at my church, when the parish prepared Greek delicacies for Resurrection's annual Greek festival, where I truly shared in the communal cooking experience. I would sign up for making *pastitsio*, *tiropites*, *spanakopita*, and the many different desserts we would sell in the festival's *kafenion*—filling my August with weekly cook-fests with other parishioners.

I would show up at the church hall promptly at nine o'clock in the morning and don the granny apron I made especially for those workdays (like my *Yaya* Eleni used to wear). The older women were already at work in their aprons, melting the butter, chopping the nuts, and setting out the worktables. After years of this, they had the assembly processes down to a science. Katena, Anna, Sophia, Chrysoula, me, and fifteen other willing volunteers would commence buttering sheets of *phyllo* and folding triangles with either spinach or cheese filling. Or we would roll out 6-inch snakes of dough and twist them into shapes for *koulourakia*, and we would form fatter dough rolls for *melomacarona* or *kourembiedes*.

It was a great way to learn from the masterful older cooks, as well as to cop a few delicious morsels when they emerged fresh from the oven.

ANGELA'S SESAME KOULOURAKIA

Yields approximately 90 cookies

Preheat oven 350 degrees

½ lb. butter
½ lb. margarine
1 cup sugar
2 tsp. vanilla
2 eggs, separated
5–6 cups flour
Sesame seeds

1. Cream butter, margarine, and sugar until light.
2. Beat in egg yolks and vanilla.
3. Add flour, mixing well with your clean hands. (Amounts of flour may change based on the brand. The dough is the right texture when you are able to mold it and it is not sticky.)
4. Mold dough into long ovals, approximately ¾ inch by 3 inches. Dip one side into the egg whites that have been beaten until fluffy. Then dip it into the sesame seeds. Place the cookie sesame-side up on a baking sheet. Press the sesame seeds into the cookies with your fingers so they will stick.
5. Bake in a 350 degree oven for 20 minutes, or until lightly browned.

We would all work for three to four hours and then break for lunch. Our bag lunches of sandwiches and fruit were always supplemented with a fresh salad or tomatoes from somebody's garden or the sweets from our morning labors. Throughout it all we spiced up the day with news of poor Marianthe's son or Helen's teenage granddaughter and the aches, pains, and various health issues of all the workers. We spoke piously about last Sunday's sermon or shared

ANGELA'S FENIKIA WITH NUTS

Yields 35–40 cookies

Preheat oven 350 degrees

DOUGH

1 egg yolk
½ cup milk
½ lb. butter, melted
3 cups flour
2 tsp. baking powder
1 tsp. cinnamon
½ tsp. ground cloves

FILLING

1 cup chopped nuts (walnuts or pecans)
2 tbsp. sugar
1 tbsp. cinnamon
1 tsp. cloves

SYRUP

1½ cups honey
1½ cups water
½ cup lemon juice

1. Beat egg yolk and milk together and mix with melted butter. Stir thoroughly.
2. Sift flour with baking powder, cinnamon, and cloves, and add gradually to the liquid mixture.
3. Knead this dough into a firm, smooth ball.
4. Take a small piece, and with your hands, spread it into a flat circle, 3½ inches in diameter.
5. Place 1 rounded teaspoon filling in the center of the circle. Fold it over to form a half circle, and seal well.
6. Place cookies on baking sheets, and bake in a 350-degree oven for 45 minutes.
7. While cookies are baking combine the ingredients for the syrup into a saucepan, and bring to boil. Boil for 10–15 minutes, until thickened.
8. When the cookies are done, remove them from the oven, and dip each in the syrup. Arrange them on a plate.

We spoke piously about last Sunday's sermon or shared Lenten recipes whenever the priest would inevitably amble by to say hello and snatch a fresh, hot cookie or two.

I threw the ingredients together in what I guessed would create the taste I wanted, held my breath, and voila!

Lenten recipes whenever the priest would inevitably amble by to say hello and snatch a fresh, hot cookie or two.

One year I volunteered to help the men bake the pastitsio. Since I was the new kid in the kitchen, they initiated me by making me the onion chopper. Even with the aid of an electric chopping machine, processing onions for fifty large pans of this Greek casserole was a lachrymose experience. I took the old timers' advice of placing a piece of bread in my mouth to staunch the tears. It helped, somewhat, although I ate five unneeded slices of bread that morning. The men were very grateful and supportive and made me a delicious lunch of crisp salad and a warm serving of the fresh baked pastitsio. I always planned to go back to help them again some day, but the thought of all those onions waiting to be chopped deterred me.

So when you make these recipes, especially the ones that demand individual pieces or elaborate layering instructions, consider inviting friends or family to help out. It's fun for everybody, makes things easier for you, and food always tastes better to your friends and family when they get to help make it.

GREEK INSPIRATION

Many of my personal Greek recipes are the result of inspiration. The source of this inspiration is from memories of different dishes my mother served me through the years, but for which there were no recipes to document so commonplace a dish. I would call her on the phone; she would quickly spell out the ingredients she used; then I would try it adding my own twist.

Until I wrote this book many of those gems still existed only in my memory and were executed through habit. I never measured the ingredients for my Greek salad dressing. I sprinkled in the spices and anointed the vegetables with a practiced feel for the right amount of oil and vinegar.

ELAINE'S LEMON ROASTED POTATOES

Yields 12 servings

Preheat oven 350 degrees

½ cup butter
¼ cup olive oil
¼–½ cup lemon juice
5 lb. potatoes, peeled and quartered
Garlic powder or granules
Salt
Pepper
Oregano

Potatoes roasted in butter and lemon, a winning combo

1. Place potatoes, in a single layer, in a large roasting pan.
2. Melt butter; add olive oil and lemon juice. Stir until mixed; then pour over the potatoes.
3. Liberally sprinkle the potatoes with garlic powder.
4. Sprinkle potatoes with salt, pepper, and oregano to taste.
5. Cover the baking pan with aluminum foil, and place in 350-degree oven. Roast the potatoes covered for 1 hour. Baste the potatoes with the lemon/butter/oil mixture every 15–20 minutes.
6. Uncover the potatoes, and bake for another hour. Baste potatoes with the lemon/butter/oil mixture every 15–20 minutes.
7. If you would like the potatoes browned, raise the temperature to 400 degrees for the last 10 minutes.

Elaine's Beet Salad

Yields 4–6 servings

Bunch of beets (approx. 3–4), with green
    tops
Garlic, either minced cloves or granules
1 part olive oil
2 parts apple cider vinegar*
Salt and pepper to taste

1. Scrub the whole beets. Do not trim off the root end, but clip off their green tops leaving 1 inch of stem. Put the beets in a pot with enough water to cover them. Boil until a fork can easily stab into the beet.
2. Rinse the green tops and steam them separately until tender.
3. Peel, then slice the beets in 1/4 inch slices. Coarsely chop the green tops. Mix them together.
4. Mix the beets and greens with garlic, salt and pepper, vinegar, and olive oil.
5. Chill before serving.

*Note

It's hard to estimate the amount of dressing needed for the salad because of the different number and sizes of beets you get in a bunch. Try 1/4 cup olive oil and 1/2 cup vinegar to dress this individual salad, or mix up 1/2-cup olive oil and 1 cup vinegar, and have it on hand to dress this and your other Greek salads.

Now my mother has left this world for a better place, unreachable even by cell phone. Any other Greek recipes I devise I must divine out of thin air or from a faint recollection of how the food might have tasted when my mother cooked it. For example, I fabricated the recipe for lemon potatoes, a Greek dish that I brought to the baby shower potluck for Noah, my stepson, and his wife, Kim. I threw

ELAINE'S FETA OMELET

Serves 3–4

4–6 eggs
1–2 tbsp. milk
1–2 tbsp. butter
¼ cup chopped onions
½ fresh tomato, chopped
Fresh or dried basil to taste
Salt and pepper and garlic powder
¼ cup feta cheese, crumbled

1. Beat 4–6 eggs with 1–2 tbsp. milk.
2. In a large frying pan, melt butter and sauté onion and tomatoes, until onion is translucent.
3. Pour in the egg mixture. Sprinkle it with salt, pepper, garlic powder, and basil, to taste.
4. Cook covered over medium low heat. When the egg mixture starts to congeal, sprinkle crumbled feta cheese across the top. Cover and cook until the egg is set and lightly brown on the bottom and the feta is slightly melted. Fold over and serve.

the ingredients together in what I guessed would create the taste I wanted, held my breath, and voila! I received many praises for the hot, lemony results.

Another recipe I created was necessitated by my desire to feed a friend who had been put on a special no salt, no fat diet. The result was the chicken or turkey kabobs, listed in Healthy Options. Once again, I used my food memory of Greek spices and cooking methods to try something new in the spur of the moment. And once again the results worked.

Even the Greek inspired broiled liver, even *that*, tastes wonderful with the aid of Greek-style spices. Long ago, when I was in Weight

Even the Greek inspired broiled liver, even that, tastes wonderful with the aid of Greek-style spices.

ELAINE'S DOLMATA SALATA

Serves 4–6

4 large fresh tomatoes
½–¾ red or yellow onion, sliced thin
½–1 cucumber, peeled
½ cup crumbled feta cheese
1–2 cloves fresh garlic, chopped or garlic
      granules to taste
½–1 tsp. dried oregano
Salt and pepper to taste
1 part olive oil*
2 parts vinegar, wine or apple cider*

1. Cut tomatoes into large wedges
    (approximately 8 pieces per tomato).
2. Add sliced onions.
3. Cut the cucumber into lengthwise
    quarters. Slice into ¼–½ inch
    slices, and add them to the rest of
    vegetables.
4. Add garlic and feta cheese, and then
    sprinkle with the oregano, salt, and
    pepper.
5. Pour the olive oil and vinegar into
    vegetable mixture and toss well.
6. Chill before serving.

Colorful, flavorful, and nutritious Dolmata
Salata

*NOTE

It's hard to estimate the amount of dressing
needed for the salad because of the
different types and sizes of tomatoes you
get in a bunch. Try ¼ cup olive oil and ½
cup vinegar to dress this individual salad, or
mix up ½ olive oil and 1 cup vinegar, and
have it on hand to dress your other Greek
salads.

ELAINE'S BROILED CALF'S LIVER

Calf's liver
Lemon juice
Salt and pepper
Oregano

1. Spread the calf's liver out flat on a broiling pan rack.

2. Squeeze or brush fresh lemon juice over the surface of the liver.
3. Sprinkle with salt, pepper, and oregano.
4. Broil the liver, turning once, until it is no longer red inside, but an even grayish-brown throughout. (Don't overcook it, or the liver will become tough.)

Watchers and the program called for liver once a week, I used that recipe. I derived it from the way my mother prepared this organ meat when I was young. My friend and diet buddy, Judy, hated liver, but she gladly ate her weekly requirement when she made it using this recipe.

So try these dishes and develop your own using the spices, combinations, and methods you have learned in this book. Who knows what wonderful foods you will create for your family and friends, inspired by the Greeks?

AVGOLEMONO SOUP

This chicken soup is a standard at most Greek restaurants and a favorite of their patrons. The tart, rich egg-lemon sauce enlivens the ordinary

ELAINE'S AVGOLEMONO SOUP

Yields 8 servings

1 whole chicken
8–10 cups water
1 onion, chopped
1 carrot, halved and sliced thin
2 stalks celery, chopped
1 cup rice
3 eggs, separated
Juice of 1 lemon
Salt and pepper to taste

Tangy egg-lemon sauce makes for a zestful chicken soup.

1. Boil the chicken and vegetables in water, until the chicken is cooked and falling off the bone (about 1 hour).
2. Remove chicken to cool, saving resulting broth. While the chicken cools, add enough water to the broth to make 8 cups of liquid.
3. Add rice, salt and pepper, and cook over medium heat, until the rice is cooked (about 25 minutes).
4. While the rice is cooking, bone and chop chicken into bite-sized pieces. Set aside until step 8.
5. Separate egg whites into a large mixing bowl, and beat until stiff. Then beat in the yolks. Add the lemon juice, and beat well.
6. Add the soup broth into the egg mixture a little at a time and very slowly, beating constantly. Do this until most of the broth has been added to

Continued on next page

the mixture. (This slow addition of hot broth into the egg mixture is necessary to avoid curdling the eggs.)

7. Then slowly pour the mixture back into the soup, stirring well.
8. Add back chicken to the soup. (There may be more cooked chicken than you need in the soup. Add as much as you like, saving the rest for sandwiches or salads.)
9. Serve immediately.

OPTIONS

- Use 2 cans of chicken rice soup for a quick way to make this soup. Warm the soup as you make the egg and lemon mixture, using 2 eggs and ⅓ less lemon juice. Then follow steps 5, 6, and 7, above.
- ♥ We occasionally add diced fresh broccoli, a delicious addition of green vegetables to the meal.

chicken and rice broth. The dish was standard fare in my house—both when I grew up and when I raised my own children. After watching me make and add the foaming egg-lemon mixture to the basic broth, Charlie and Sally loved eating a steaming bowl of soup for supper with Greek bread and butter, feta cheese, and olives. My grandchildren love it as well.

Its preparation is also versatile. Add more chicken and you make a heartier meal. If you are in a hurry, use canned chicken and rice soup as a base, and bring the cooking time down to heating the soup and adding the egg-lemon ingredients. And if you're serving this dish to your in-laws, you might be surprised at what they choose to add. Art Schmitz, my father-in-law, loved the soup after he sprinkled his bowlful with dried onion flakes and stirred in a large dollop of catsup!

If you're serving this dish to your in-laws, you might be surprised at what they choose to add.

KOTA KAPAMA: MY NEW TRADITIONAL BIRTHING MEAL

Most of the culinary traditions I observe come from my mother and grandmothers, especially when the dish is Greek. The few exceptions to them are the traditions that I have started. Making *Kota Kapama,* when my children become parents and I first visit them to celebrate and meet our new grandchild, has become one of my traditions. I'm not sure whether there is some archetypal symbolism in a chicken stew or, perhaps, a deeper nutritional imperative that suggested it to me. I just know I like it, and it feels like the right thing to do.

I started this practice when I made the stew for Sally, my daughter, and her husband, Eric, after Lila, our first grandchild, was born. Well, maybe it wasn't the first time I met Lila, but I pulled the recipe out of my archives while she was still an infant. Then her sister Rubini was born, and when I visited to attend her birth, I made the dish for the family again. By the time Asher, our first grandson, came into the world, it had become my tradition. Therefore, when I traveled to Denver to meet Asher and to help while his parents, Charlie and Susan, settled into their new roles, I made this delicious dish. And the stew was served again when Maranatha was born.

Kota Kapama is tasty comfort food to me. A hearty dish of chicken, noodles, and a savory sauce, it fills the house with a redolent aroma as it cooks. It is sweet and rich, with plenty of protein and carbohydrates. Made the traditional way, the stew also contains a fair amount of healthy fat, something I feel justified serving a nursing mother. For those of us who aren't nursing mothers, I have provided lower fat alternatives to the recipe.

So this *Yaya* makes *Kota Kapama* to celebrate new life and new additions to the family. May (s)he live for us! *Na mas zisi!*

Kota Kapama is tasty comfort food to me. A hearty dish of chicken, noodles, and a savory sauce, it fills the house with a redolent aroma as it cooks.

ANGELA'S KOTA KAPAMA

Yields 4–6 servings

1 large chicken, cut into serving pieces
Salt and pepper
Ground cinnamon
4 tbsp. olive oil
2 tbsp. butter
15-oz. can of stewed or diced tomatoes
6-oz. can tomato paste
¾ cup water
3 sticks cinnamon
2 medium onions, finely chopped
3–5 cloves garlic, minced
1 large onion, studded with whole cloves
1 lb. macaroni or spaghetti
Grated Parmesan or Romano cheese

1. Sprinkle the chicken pieces with salt, pepper, and cinnamon.
2. Brown the pieces on both sides in 2 tbsp. of olive oil a large *katsarola* (electric frying pan or Dutch oven).
3. In a separate pan, brown the chopped onions and minced garlic in 2 tbsp. olive oil.
4. Combine the tomatoes, tomato paste, and water with the onions and garlic, and pour the sauce over the browned chicken pieces.
5. Add the cinnamon sticks and a whole peeled onion into which you have spiked whole cloves at about ¾ inch intervals.
6. Bring the mixture to a boil, and then lower the heat and cover, simmering the chicken until tender.
7. Cook the pasta according to the directions on the package; drain.
8. Brown 2 tbsp. of butter in the pasta pan, and toss the drained pasta into the butter. You can either add the pasta to the chicken dish or add the sauce from the chicken to it and serve it on the side.

OPTIONS

For a leaner dish try the following:

♥ After browning the chicken drain the fat, reserving 2 tbsp. in which to sauté the onions and garlic.

Continued on next page

♥ Skin the chicken before seasoning and browning.

♥ Omit the 2 tbsp. of butter in the pasta, adding the pasta directly to the tomato sauce after draining.

■ From my mother's notes: You can substitute potatoes for the pasta, eliminating the clove-studded onion. With this option you will peel and quarter 4–6 potatoes, adding them to the simmering chicken to cook.

ROASTED CHESTNUTS

Irina exclaimed, "Oh, chestnuts!" Looking down I recognized them, and my memory was flooded with the taste and texture of the hot, roasted nut.

On a recent crisp October day, I was walking in the old city of Chartres, France, with Irina, a friend of ours who is originally from Russia. As we went, we trod on prickly green pods beneath the spreading boughs of ancient trees that lined our way. I was too distracted by the outline of the tall, imposing cathedral against the skyline of the medieval town to notice the fat brown nuts that had been ejected from the trod-upon pods, until Irina exclaimed, "Oh, chestnuts!" Looking down I recognized them, and my memory was flooded with the taste and texture of the hot, roasted nut.

My mother used to make them for us in the winter, as well as using them in the Greek stuffing she served on Thanksgiving. She also loved to tell us stories of how my *Papou* Peter sold cones of the toasty nuts from his snack shack.

Nowadays we listen to recordings of Johnny Mathis singing the "Christmas Song" every year, proclaiming the warmth and coziness of chestnuts roasting on an open fire. But does anybody roast and eat them anymore, that is, except for my stepson, Darshan, and me? I believe chestnuts may have lost the battle of the snacks to salty chips or the gooey, heavily sugared, mainly chocolate offerings that have become the modern world's traditional winter treats.

ANGELA'S
ROASTED CHESTNUTS

1. Prepare any number of chestnuts by scoring an X with a knife through the tough brown coat on the rounded upper part of the nut.
2. Place in a pan, with a little water in the bottom of it (just enough to cover the bottom of the pan).
3. Roast in a 425-degree oven for 20 minutes.
4. Serve the roasted nuts immediately. Cut or peel off the inner brown coat before eating.

To me, chestnuts are an old world delicacy. When Steven and I visited Athens, Greece, we bought a cone of them from one of the street vendors whose stands dot the shopping areas of the city. The warm, nutty aroma attracted us like bees to honey. The sweet, earthy taste filtered into our mouths as we chewed the sticky, soft nuts. I have never found a chestnut street vendor in all my American travels.

In the New World, chestnuts are more nostalgia than substance, like the roasted apples and walnuts Louisa May Alcott wrote about in *Little Women*. At that time oranges on Christmas morning were a treasure, a cause for celebration. Nature's bounty, simply served, could satisfy the tummy and the taste buds. Many times these old traditions can be revived. Try this easy recipe and recapture the taste of a merry, old holiday season—simply served.

MY FRENCH COUSIN

It amazes me that I have a French cousin, Gabrielle Carlos Le Quere, who lives outside of Paris in a small town on the Seine with her husband, Jean Marc, and the youngest of their four children, Logan. To me she is evidence of a mysterious and playful universe.

How did this happen? It is a story of a World War, an untimely death, and a little girl who was sent back to live with her grandparents in Paris when she was eight years old. My Aunt Henriette was a war bride. My Uncle Angelo, my mother's brother, met her in France after that country's liberation in World War II. They married in the dizzying aftermath, and he took her home to his family in Detroit, Michigan.

During a tempestuous and all too brief marriage, Henriette gave birth to Gabrielle, who is less than three years younger than me. I remember her as a sweet little pixie with bright eyes, curly hair, and frilly dresses. When she was four and my Uncle was thirty-two, he died of a massive coronary—the result of a weakened heart from a childhood bout of rheumatic fever and lots of overtime at work. Suddenly Gabrielle was gone, too, when my aunt and she moved to New York, to live with my Aunt's brother.

I was seven at the time of my Uncle's death, so I lost track of her. Later, I heard she had moved to France. She dropped from my awareness until I was married and eight months pregnant with Sally. Then, when she was twenty-one, she showed up with our cousin Brian in tow. Brian was twenty-one at the time, too, and no longer fell off teeter-totters, but he did fall for Gabrielle. They were on a harem-scarem adventure that had started in Detroit, when she went to visit Aunt Kathryn after she graduated from the Sorbonne, and ended at our doorstep, where we had a front row seat to the proceedings. She was a beautiful, saucy young French girl, and Brian was proud that she took him along with her on her travels. During their visit with us, the two of them talked themselves out of a traffic ticket when Brian let

I remember her as a sweet little pixie with bright eyes, curly hair, and frilly dresses.

Gabrielle's Pilaf

Yields 6–8 servings

¼ cup butter
½ cup orzo pasta
1 cup raw white rice
3 cups chicken or turkey broth
½–¾ tsp. salt
¼ tsp. white pepper

1. Brown the rice and orzo in butter.
2. Add the rest of the ingredients and bring to boil. Simmer for 20–25 minutes (or until the pasta and rice are dry and fluffy).

Notes

- This is a very basic yet tasty pilaf. It can be embellished with garlic, mushrooms, oregano, and toasted almonds or pine nuts.
- Or try substituting the broth noted above with only 2 cups of the chicken or turkey broth and an 8-oz. can of tomato sauce.

Versatile pilaf complements almost any meal

Gabrielle drive one day in Coronado, California (where I lived). She had traveled the wrong way for several blocks down a one-way street, which was a major thoroughfare to the island's Naval Air Station.

The next time I saw her was seventeen years later, when I went to Europe with my college-aged son, Charlie. She had become a doctor, married another doctor, and was pregnant with the last of her four children. Her husband, Jean Marc, proved a wonderful tour guide, and they regaled us with the sights in and around Paris for three days. I had to blast Charlie out of there; he was enthralled with Jean Marc, who was quite a bon vivant.

I've seen her only twice since then. The last time was when we traveled to France recently for an international conference at which my husband, Steven, spoke. We had dinner with Gabrielle and her husband in Montmartre. She is still very beautiful and now, very French; although, when I look at her, I can see the features of my Greek family echoed in her face. And Jean Marc is still a very delightful and knowledgeable tour guide. I am happy to include a French-Greek dish in this volume, from the kitchen of my cousin, Gabrielle.

HEALTHY OPTIONS

Mediterranean food has recently been touted for its heart healthy effects, and for good reason. The pervasive use of olive oil—a monosaturated fat, the abundance of fresh vegetables, and the many recipes that feature fish all contribute to this benefit.

And then there are those other recipes that seem to belie this worthy reputation. They include *baklava, galatoboureko, pastitsio*—the ones that call for pounds of butter, fried ingredients, rich sauces, and red meat. What's up? My family has given this much thought, especially since we are prone to overindulge. And I have come to the conclusion that the health benefits of Greek food are a matter of cultural context as much as content.

I have come to the conclusion that the health benefits of Greek food are a matter of cultural context as much as content.

ELAINE'S CHICKEN AND TURKEY TENDERS KEBABS

Yields 4 servings

1 lb. chicken or turkey tenders
Juice of 1 lemon
¼ cup white wine
¼ cup olive oil
Garlic powder or granules
Oregano
Salt and pepper
1 onion, quartered with layers separated
Green and red pepper pieces, cherry
   tomatoes, and mushrooms

1. Cut tenders into 1-inch cubes and place them in a deep bowl. Mix lemon juice, wine and olive oil, and pour over the tenders.
2. Sprinkle the tenders with garlic, oregano, and salt and pepper to taste, and toss the tenders to mix the spices into the liquid marinade and coat the meat pieces.
3. Press onion pieces on top of the meat, and place a heavy dish on top of them.
4. Place the meat in the refrigerator for at least 2 hours to one day before cooking.
5. One hour before serving, remove the onions to a plate and mix tenders and marinade thoroughly.
6. Place poultry and onions, tomatoes, green and red peppers, and mushrooms in random order on skewers.
7. Barbecue over medium heat, or broil for 20–25 minutes, turning the skewers and basting with the marinade often. Cook until the meat is thoroughly done.

NOTES

- Depending on diet issues, both the wine and olive oil are optional. Just increase the lemon juice to that of 2 lemons.
- Carefully remove the ingredients from the skewers to avoid crushing the tomatoes, which with pressure will spit out their pulp and seeds.

Marinated poultry with fresh cut vegetables, a tasty and healthy choice

Kathryn's Meatless Eggplant Casserole

Yields 4 servings

Preheat oven 350 degrees

Salt
Flour
1 egg
1 cup low or non-fat milk
1 medium eggplant, peeled and cut into
    1/4 inch slices
Dry, unseasoned bread crumbs
Canola oil (for frying)
1/3–1/2 lb. or more shredded skim-milk
    mozzarella
2 tbsp. grated Parmesan or Romano
    cheese

Sauce

1 tbsp. olive oil
1 medium onion, finely chopped
1 or more cloves garlic, minced
1 (1 lb. 12 oz.) can diced tomatoes
Salt and pepper to taste
1/4 rounded tsp. dried oregano
1/2 rounded tsp. dried basil
1/2 lb. fresh mushrooms, sliced (optional)
1/2 cup white wine (optional)

1. Make sauce: in a 2-quart saucepan, cook the onion and garlic until soft. Add mushrooms to the sauté, and cook until soft before adding the rest of the ingredients. Stir and simmer, uncovered for 1 hour.
2. Salt the peeled eggplant slices, and place them in a colander. Weigh them down with a heavy plate or lid for 30 minutes. Pat them dry with paper towel.
3. Mix flour and salt together.
4. Beat together egg and milk.
5. Dip eggplant slices in flour mix, then in egg mixture, then in breadcrumbs. Refrigerate the coated eggplant in the refrigerator for about 1/2 hour.
6. Fry the slices in hot oil (medium heat) until golden brown, and then drain on paper towel.
7. Grease a 9 x 9 inch casserole dish, and arrange a layer of half of the sliced eggplant in the bottom of the pan. Cover with mozzarella cheese, and sprinkle with grated cheese. Top with

Continued on next page

half of the sauce. Repeat layers, ending with another layer of mozzarella cheese.

8. Bake in the preheated 350 degree oven for 40 minutes or until cheese is melted.

NOTE

- If you double the recipe, you will still need only 1 egg and ½ cup milk in which to dip the eggplant. Use an 11 x 15 x 2 inch pan.

♥ I successfully made a wheat-free, gluten-free version of this dish, substituting brown rice flour for wheat flour and using Ener-G gluten-free, wheat-free bread crumbs.

Consider that ninety-eight percent of the population in Greece belongs to the Greek Orthodox Church. The Church directs its members to fast or abstain from all but vegetables, fruits, grains, and shellfish for what adds up to over fifty percent of the year. It also prescribes strict practices of abstinence, traditionally requiring that during fasts, the faithful eat only one meal in the late afternoon. This directive greatly influenced everyday diets in historical Greece.

Consider that for hundreds of years, Greece was a poor nation. Many people were sequestered on small islands in the middle of the Mediterranean, living off of what the poor soil and the boundless sea could provide. So, many of the rich dishes in this book were causes for celebration. They were the feasts that balanced the fasting and famine.

When the Greeks moved to America, they found abundance, which provided them with the ability to eat the special, rich dishes more often. Being hospitable people, they fed their friends these luscious delicacies whenever they came to call. At the same time, fasting practices diminished, sometimes entirely. So my hardy family ancestors gave way to those fighting many private battles of the bulges.

We fought these battles by revising the traditional recipes in ways that preserved the authentic taste, but omitted saturated fats and sugar.

My mother started to make many of these substitutions in order to manage my father's waistline and health. He lived to the age of 85, so I believe she was successful in that challenge. In this book I have included many original healthy cuisine recipes and those that are fast-worthy. I have also included healthier options to many of the traditional recipes. The two in this section are examples of dishes we've recreated to eliminate as much animal fat as possible. So, to your health, or as the Greeks would say, "*Yassas!*"

With love, to the next generations.

The Baton Passes

LAMB BURGERS: THE NEXT GENERATION

My family's cuisine was imported to America at the beginning of the last century. It has survived and evolved for 100 years. Now, in the early twenty-first century, it is important to me that this legacy is passed on to my children and grandchildren. At this time the group includes one son, one daughter, two stepsons, their wives and husbands, and seven grandchildren. My family also contains a blessed number of surviving aunts and uncles, and numerous cousins and their spouses and sons and daughters. I am happy to report that these recipes are still sought after among this number.

My cousin Nick and I traded recipes in preparation for this book, his *loukoumades* recipe for my secret cookie recipe. My daughter, Sally, regularly calls me with variations of the question, "How do you make *Yaya's* . . . ?" (Fill in baked chicken or rice pudding, or the latest request, *dolmadakia*.) All of the children love it when I serve them one of these recipes on our visits to their homes. They and their spouses are great cooks of Greek food, too.

When Noah was studying at University of Heidelberg, he met his father and me in Athens, where Steven and I were celebrating our fourth anniversary. Together we toured the Parthenon, marveling at the massive marble columns, the carved stone friezes, and its museum of golden artifacts. We shopped for icons and souvenirs in Plaka, the

In a prime example of nurture over nature, I have included the following recipe from my stepson, Noah Schmitz, a connoisseur of Greek cooking.

NOAH'S LAMB BURGERS

Ground lamb (⅓–½ lbs. per person)
Salt and pepper, to taste
Worcestershire sauce, 1 tbsp. for each lb.
    of meat
Soy sauce, 3 tsp. for each lb. of meat
Olive oil, 1 tbsp. for each lb. of meat
Chopped fresh garlic, at least 1 clove per
    lb. of meat
Dash of cayenne powder
Crumbled feta cheese or spreadable goat
    cheese
Olive tapenade
Hamburger buns

1. Put ground lamb in a mixing bowl.
2. Knead in salt, pepper, Worcestershire
   sauce, soy sauce, olive oil, garlic, and
   cayenne.
3. Form separate patties. Dimple the
   middle of each patty so that they
   cook flat instead of bulging into a ball.

4. Grill the patties until done to your
   liking.
5. While the patties are cooking, toast the
   burger buns.
6. To serve: Spread a tbsp of olive
   tapenade on each toasted bun. Place a
   patty on each bun and place a tbsp. of
   finely crumbled feta or spreadable goat
   cheese onto each patty. Cover the patty
   with the top bun and enjoy.

OPTIONS

♥ Although lamb provides you with the
   most authentic Greek taste, the burgers
   are also delicious if you use ground
   beef, buffalo, or turkey meat. Buffalo and
   turkey will be your leanest option.
♥ If you like the crunch of raw vegetables
   with your burgers, add lettuce leaves,
   sliced tomatoes, and onion slices to the
   sandwiches.

ancient Athenian marketplace. Noah, with his blond good looks, had an entourage of admiring Greek cuties following us as we wound our way through its cobblestone streets. The three of us also sampled the wonderful Greek fare at the *estiatoria* (restaurants) throughout the city. We tried the *moussaka, spanakopita, tiropites,* and lots of *baklava*.

One day we went to the Temple of Poseidon at Sounion, some miles beyond Piraeus. The beautiful ruin was perched on a craggy cliff overlooking the rugged coast of the Aegean Sea. Our view included meadows of lush green grass and early spring wildflowers, and the silver gray columns that still stood tall against a deep blue sky. We had driven there in a hired taxi over the windy bluffs along the coast. In one of the little beachside towns we stopped for lunch at a large bakery, which featured sandwiches of fresh sliced tomatoes and feta cheese thickly spread on crusty Greek bread. I was impressed by how Noah devoured the sharp, salty sandwiches with the same gusto as I. Through the years since, he has even featured crumbled feta in his guacamole, so it didn't surprise me to hear that he had devised this hamburger recipe. In a sense, the family cuisine has come full circle, or should I say, in a spiral—similar to the old ways yet made with new ingredients for modern tastes. I think my *Papou* Peter would have approved of this burger, with its inspired use of traditional Greek ingredients of ground lamb and feta cheese.

MY GRANDMOTHER'S SECRET COOKIE RECIPE

"Please, Angie, we love these cookies. We've been family for over 20 years. Can't you teach us how to make them?" my aunts pleaded.

"I'm not sure," my mother replied. "You're my husband's side of the family. The recipe is from my side of the family. My family used to make their livelihood with these cookies. I don't think my mother would like it if I gave the secret over to the Manolakas side."

"My family used to make their livelihood with these cookies. I don't think my mother would like it if I gave the secret over to the Manolakas side."

"Ang, your mother's been dead for 5 years. The cookie business stopped when your father died 35 years ago. All your nieces and nephews love the cookies. Please, won't you just teach us the recipe?"

They had been over this ground many times before. My aunts would beg, and my mother would withhold, savoring the power she had over them. So I think it surprised us all when sometime in the 1970s she relented, saying, "Well, if I do, you have to swear that you won't tell anybody outside of the family how to make them. And they're only to be made by you."

My aunts were begging my mom to teach them to make the Greek *koulouria* my grandfather had sold from his snack shack. The shack stood in front of his house and next to the Greek Church and school, a prime location for his wares. That secret Greek cookie was his specialty and most lucrative product.

Sally, Charles, and Susan mix secret cookie ingredients, 2002.

My grandmother helped him by making the *koulouria* from the recipe they bought from a French baker in 1915 for $500. The price included the oven, pans, and mixing equipment. It's an old, odd recipe with ingredients that might seem unusual by today's tastes. There are no chocolate chips or chunks in it, no marshmallows, no peanut butter nougat, but the cookies are good anyway, regardless of time and place.

Since the recipe is a secret I will share one distinguishing ingredient, *masticha*. Unmistakably Greek, they are little drops of pine resin, resembling pale beads of amber. The resin is from pine trees that grow exclusively on the southwestern coast of Chios, the Greek island of my father's family. The Greeks prize the organic, musty taste of these drops; they grind them up and add the *masticha* to breads, cookies, drinks, and even chewing gum. Like biscotti, there is nothing better than to dunk these cookies in a cup of strong, hot coffee, especially with lots of milk and sugar in it.

My mother finally relented and shared the secret with her three sisters-in-law, Betty, Ginny, and Chubby. Shortly thereafter all who now knew the recipe started experimenting with laborsaving ways to make the cookies. They used rolling pins and doughnut cutters to form the circular shapes, instead of rolling out and shaping tubes of dough. They also started tweaking the ingredients. These innovations were heresy to me.

Despite that distant breach the recipe has remained a family secret. Of all my cousins, I was the only direct descendant who had been entrusted with the original recipe and taught how to make it. Many years and a new millennium later it dawned on me: there are only four women now alive who know the recipe, me and three ladies in their 70s and 80s. If the recipe was to be passed on it was up to me, and I had better act quickly.

So I introduced Sally, Charlie, my stepson Darshan, and Susan (who married Charlie in 2004) to the family secret in the summer of 2002, when they all came home for Noah's and Kim's wedding. Along with a copy of the recipe, I gave them a cooking lesson. What they learned, along with what to add and how, was that their mother hadn't made the cookies in so long she had forgotten how.

If they were taking detailed notes the first part of the lesson would have looked like this:

1. Decide to make only half the recipe and quickly revise the amounts in your head. Have each person add half of one ingredient.
2. When it comes to the butter, dispute the amount with your son, Charlie. Win the argument, confusing and irritating him.
3. Then after he adds it and it's creamed into the dry ingredients, notice that the mixture looks much too greasy. Ruefully

Elaine, Lila, Darshan, Charles, Susan, and Sally make the secret cookies, 2002.

Now that the secrecy had been breached and the recipe had been shared, they all felt they could change it.

*"Circles are boring,"
he announced as he
formed a big, sloppy,
misshapen pretzel from
a lump of dough.*

announce that *we* made a mistake. Charlie actually added the amount needed for the full recipe.

4. Have each child add his or her ingredient again to balance the recipe, except Charlie—who was right in the first place.

At one point we had to mush our hands into the ingredients to mix the liquid into the dry by hand, creating sticky dough that clung to our fingers like glue. The five of us had the flour, sugar, and milk mixture creeping up our arms, across our faces, and into our hair.

We made the cookies so big and fat that we only formed about 70—half of the expected yield. (Maybe the doughnut cutters my aunts had introduced would have been a good idea to use.) During the process Darshan and Sally, the artists in the family, started taking liberties with the shapes. Darshan instigated this sacrilege. I squawked in protest, but everybody had stopped listening to me after I miscalculated the butter.

Then Sally said, "Cool, I want to try it, too," and she started making snakes and pretzels. Then the others fashioned blobs and snakes and pretzels, laughing at the odd assortment of shapes they crafted. I diligently stayed true to tradition and continued making the circles, dismayed at the youthful rebellion in my kitchen.

I think I need to follow up on the lessons with further practice and individual lectures on the importance of tradition. Or maybe I will just wait and entrust the recipe to my grandchildren, who will surely appreciate their *Yaya's* mystery more than their modern, rebellious parents do.

ELENI'S COOKIES

It's a family secret! You didn't really think I would give this out to the world.

But to make it up to you, here's another wonderful Greek cookie for you to try. It's one of my favorites.

Angela's Melomacarona

Yields 60–70 cookies

Preheat oven 375 degrees

1 cup butter
1½ cup vegetable oil
½ cup sugar
2 tbsp. whiskey
Grated rind of 1 orange
Juice of 1 orange and ½ lemon
    (approximately ½ cup liquid)
2 tsp. baking soda
1 cup finely chopped nuts
¼ tsp. ground cloves
¼ tsp. cinnamon
Approximately 6–7 cups flour

Syrup

2 cups honey
1 cup water
1 cup finely chopped nuts

1. Melt the butter and let it cool.
2. Put the butter in a mixer, and add the vegetable oil. Beat until creamy.
3. Add sugar, and beat thoroughly.

Melomacarona: Honey dipped, nut-filled delight

4. Add juices and whiskey, rind, baking soda, spices, and 1 cup of the nuts. Mix well.
5. Add the flour, a little at a time, until a medium-soft, smooth dough, is formed.
6. Take about a tbsp. of the dough and roll it into an egg shape. Flatten the bottom a little, and place on ungreased cookie

Continued on next page

sheet. Press the top of each cookie with a fork to make indentations to hold the chopped nuts.

7. Bake in a 375-degree oven for 30–35 minutes.

8. While the cookies are baking, make the syrup by boiling 2 cups honey and 1 cup water for a few minutes.

9. After the cookies have baked and are still warm, dip them into the syrup, and place on a plate. Sprinkle them with the second cup of the finely chopped nuts.

OPTIONS

- For an alcohol-free cookie, substitute the orange juice, lemon juice, and whiskey with ⅔ cup orange juice.
- Sprinkle with cinnamon and sugar instead of the chopped nuts.

Recipe Index

APPETIZERS

Keftaides, Despina's	The Yaya Wars	37
Roasted Chestnuts, Angela's	Roasted Chestnuts	165
Taramasalata, Angela's	Angela's Entertaining	106
Taramasalata, Kathryn's	Easter Revisited	89
Tiropites, Eleni's	More Summer Cooking	59

SOUPS

Avgolemeno, Elaine's	Avgolemono Soup	160
Fahki, Angela	The Straw, the Bean, and the Coal	67

SALADS

Beet Salad, Elaine's	Greek Inspiration	156
Dolmata Salata, Elaine's	Greek Inspiration	158
Greek Salad, Angela's	Greek Salad	127
Four Bean Salad, Angela's	Four Bean Salad	129

VEGETABLES AND LENTEN DISHES

Bamias, Tootsie's	Lost Recipes	121
Candied Yams, Angela's	Thanksgiving	74
Dandelion Leaves, Elaine	Foraging for Food	149

Fassolakia, Angela's   More Summer Cooking   62
Fassolourizo, Angela's   The Straw, the Bean, and
                                              the Coal   66
Lemon Roasted Potatoes, Elaine's   Greek Inspiration   155
Spanakorizo, Angela's   Kitchen Capers   69
Tourlou, Angela's   Angela's Entertaining   108

POULTRY AND EGGS

Baked Chicken Oregani, Angela's   My Mother Learns to Cook   44
Chicken and Turkey Tenders Kebabs, Elaine's   Healthy Options   169
Chicken Pilafi, Angela's   My Mother Learns to Cook   43
Eggs with Zucchini, Angela's   Every Day Fare   101
Feta Omelet, Elaine's   Greek Inspiration   157
Greek Barbequed Chicken, Connie's   Summertime Barbeque   51
Kota Kapama, Angela's   My New Traditional
                                              Birthing Meal   163

MEATS

Arni Souvlakia, Connie   Summertime Barbeque   50
Broiled Calves Liver, Elaine's   Greek Inspiration   159
Dolmadakia me Avgolemeno, Despina's   Foraging for Food   147
Greek Stuffing, Eleni's   Thanksgiving   78
Hamburgers, Peter Carlos' Snack Shop   Peter Carlos' Snack Shop
                                              Burgers   10
Lamb and Orzo Roasted in the Pan, Angela's   Ang's Entertaining   133
Lamb Burgers, Noah's   The Baton Passes   176
Roast Leg of Lamb, Angela's   Ang's Entertaining   132
Yankee Pot Roast, Angela's   Yankee Pot Roast   146
Youvarlakia, Eleni's   Every Day Fare   99

FISH

Broiled or Barbequed Fish, Connie's   Summertime Barbeque   52
Psari Plaki, Angela's   My Dad the Sailor   104

CASSEROLES AND PITAS

Meatless Eggplant Casserole, Kathryn's	Healthy Options	171
Moussaka, Angela's	Ang's Entertaining	111
Pastitsio, Angela's	More Summer Cooking	54
Spanakopita, Angela's	Ang's Entertaining	109
Spanakopita, Kathryn's	Easter Revisited	91
Stuffed Tomatoes and Green Peppers, Angela's	More Summer Cooking	56
Zucchini Casserole, Angela's	Angela's Entertaining	107

PASTAS AND PILAFS

Greek Side Dish Pasta, Angela's	Every Day Fare	100
Pilaf, Gabriella's	My French Cousin	167

DESSERTS AND HOLIDAY BREAD

Baklava, Eleni's	The Yaya Wars	38
Copenheim, Minnie's	Lost Recipes	125
Fenikia with Nuts, Angela's	Communal Cooking	153
Galatoboureko, Eleni's	Recipe Creep	143
Galatoboureko, Kathryn's	Easter Revisited	93
Galatoboureko. Angela's	Recipe Creep	144
Kallitsounakia, Eleni's	Cretan Cooking	17
Karidopeta, Maritza's	My Brother and Sister-In-Law	137
Karidopeta, Chubby's	Lost Recipes	122
Kolokithopita, Tootsie's	Many Lost Recipes	119
Koulourakia, Eleni's	My Greek Kitchen	140
Koulourakia, Kathryn's	Easter Revisited	95
Koulourakia, Stamatia's	Visiting My Old Auntie	32
Kourambeides, Angela's	Christmas	81
Kourambeides, Eleni's	Christmas	80
Loukoumades, Despina's	Loukoumades	25
Melomacarona, Angela's	Eleni's Secret Cookie Recipe	181
Paximadia, Despina's	Paximadia	27
Peach Cobbler, Angela's	More Summer Cooking	61

Ravani, Poula's	My Brother and Sister-In-Law	135
Rice Pudding, Angela's	Rice Pudding	130
Sesame Koulourakia, Angela's	Communal Cooking	152
Theples, Despina's	Lost Recipes	124
Vasilopita and Pascha Kouloures, Eleni's	New Year's	83

SAUCES, CONDIMENTS, PRESERVES, MISC.

Grapefruit Spoon Sweets, Eleni's	Glieko	7
Fig Preserves, Angela's	A Fig Jam	117
Skordalia, Minnie's	Lost Recipes	123
Summer Sunday Lunch	Sunday Lunch	114
Yaourti, Eleni's	Easter	86
Cranberry Sauce, Angela's	Thanksgiving	75
Turkey Gravy, Eleni's	Thanksgiving	76

Cast of Characters

Recipe Contributors Noted in Italic

THE CARLOS FAMILY

Peter Carlos	My mother's father and my Papou
Eleni Foumaki Carlos	My mother's mother and my Yaya

Their Children

Constantine (Gus) Carlos	Married Ellen; children: Perry, Paul, Georgia (Gigi)
Angela Carlos Manolakas (Angie)	Married Constantine; children: Stanton, *Elaine*
William (Billy) Carlos	
Angelo Carlos	Married Henriette; child: *Gabrielle*
Kathryn Carlos Backos	Married Donald; children: Sanford (Sandy), Brian

MY YAYA ELENI'S SISTER IN AMERICA:

Mary Foumaki Proimos	Married Tony Proimos; children: Kathryn, Tony, Loula, many more I can't name

THE MANOLAKAS FAMILY

Stamatios Manolakas (Sam)	My father's father, my Papou
Despina Vlisides Manolakas	My father's mother, my Yaya

Their Children

Constantine Manolakas (Connie)	Married Angela; children: Stanton, *Elaine*
George Manolakas	Married Betty; children: Thomas (Sam), Dale, Linda (Peachy), George, Robert (Bobby)
Elias (Lee) Manolakas	Married *Katherine (Chubby);* children: Sam (Butchie), Stefan, Stacy
Eugenia Manolakas Papageorge (Ginny)	Married George; child: Nicholas (Nicky)

MY PAPOU STAMATIOS' BROTHER IN AMERICA

Mike Manolakas	Married *Stamatia;* children: George, Alex, Sotiri (Teddy)

MY YAYA DESPINA'S BROTHERS AND SISTER IN AMERICA

Gus Vlisides	Widowed; child: Angela
Chris Vlisides	Married Elena; children: George, Elias, Dolly
Jim Vlisides	Married Victoria; child: Tina
Steve Vlisides	Married Vasso; children: Elias, Angela (Beetsa), Peter, Nick, and Bill
Sophia Vlisides Pettikas	Married Leonidas (Yondi); children: Angela, Irene, Olga, Tom, Elias

MY CURRENT NUCLEAR FAMILY

Stanton Manolakas	My brother, married *Barbara*
Elaine Manolakas Hawes Schmitz	The author, mother of Charles, Sarah (Sally)
Steven Schmitz	My husband, father of Noah, Darshan
Charles Hawes (Charlie or Chuck)	My son, married Susan; children: Asher, Maranatha
Sarah Hawes Smith (Sally)	My daughter, married Eric; children: Lila, Rubini (Rubi)
Noah Schmitz	My step-son, married Kim; children: Isaac, Natasha
Darshan Schmitz	My step-son, married Azusa; child: Kai

Glossary of Terms

Chronia Polla: Literally many years, a greeting on New Year's Day and Birthdays

Cross Oneself; To Do or Make the Sign of the Cross: Similar to the Catholics, Greek Orthodox believers make the sign of the cross during prayer. They use their right hands, putting their thumb, index and middle finger tips together and touch, in the following order, their foreheads, chests, right shoulders, and left shoulders.

Dolmades or Dolmadakia: Stuffed grape leaves

Estiatorio: Restaurant

Glieko: Spoon sweet; a whole fruit, flower, or fruit peel preserve

Kala Christouyenna: Merry Christmas

Kali Orexi: Good Appetite

Kafenion: Coffee house

Katsarola: A large cooking pot, like a soup kettle or Dutch oven

Koulouria: Bread

Koulourakia: Cookies

Koutala: Spoon

Kouzina: Kitchen

Loukoumi: A Greek candy, gelatinous and thinly coated with a film of confectioner's sugar

Mahlepi: An aromatic spice made from St. Lucie cherry pits. It is used in Greek holiday sweet breads, cakes, and cookies.

Makaria: The traditional meal Greeks serve at funerals to bless and celebrate the dearly departed

Mastiha: A Greek flavoring; round pearls of hard sap harvested from pine trees that grow in one part of the island of Chios; also used in making chewing gum, liquor, vitamin supplements, toothpaste

Mitera: Mother

Morae: Morons or dummies

Na mas zisi: "May he or she live for us," a congratulatory greeting at births and baptisms. This is said among family members only. For acquaintances the phrase is "Na sas zisis."

Opa: Greek term of exuberance, used to cheer dancers to amazing feats

Papa: Priest

Papou: Grandfather

Parakalo: Please

Patera: Father

Patrida: The old country; it could be Greece or one's particular city, village, or island

Phyllo Dough: also spelled Filo; pastry dough that is thin enough to resemble parchment; used for pitas and desserts

Souvlakia: Shish kebabs, traditionally made of marinated lamb, skewered and barbecued

Tarama: Red fish roe used in making taramasalata; also known as Greek caviar

Thea: Aunt

Tora: Now

Troyete: The command to Eat!

Yassas or Yassou: To your health

Yaya or Yiayia: Grandmother

Resources

Many Greek products, like feta cheese and phyllo dough, can be found in your local supermarket. They are also available from food stores specializing in Middle Eastern products. The following Internet sites also carry the ingredients listed in my recipes:

- www.krinos.com: Krinos Food Incorporated; lists many products and recipes and directing you to http://shamra.com to buy its products.
- http://www.athensfoods.com: Athens Filo (Phyllo) Dough. Helps locate stores near you to buy its products.
- http://www.greekshops.com/index.aspx: Greekshops.com. Sells many different Greek products; select "Spices, Herbs and Extracts" to find Krinos Imported Mastic gum, the mastiha used in many desserts. The small jar should last you for years.
- www.greekinternetmarket.com./groceries: Greekinternetmarket. com. Sells Tarama, pickled grape leaves, and mastiha.
- Also for Greek groceries and products: www.greekimportsinc .com/com/greek.swf, www.greekmarket.com, www.christosmarket.com, www.greecefoods.com
- www.greekwine.gr and http://duvinfinewines.com for Greek wines.

Bibliography

BOOKS

A Guide to Greek Traditions and Customs in America, by Marilyn Rouvelas, Attica Press, Bethesda, Maryland, 1994.

Cretan Cooking: The Miracle of the Cretan Diet, by Maria and N. Psilakis, Karmanor, Heraklion, Crete, circa 1995.

Hellenic Cuisine: A Collection of Greek Recipes, Editors: Mary Pyrros Karay and Fannie C. Nome, St. Helen's Philoptochos Society and Sts. Constantine and Helen Parent-Teacher Association, Detroit, Michigan, 1957.

Secrets of Fat-Free Greek Cooking, by Elaine Gavalas, Avery Publishing Group, Garden City Park, New York, 1998.

The Art of Greek Cookery, by the Women of St. Paul's Greek Orthodox Church, Hampstead, Long Island, New York, Doubleday and Company, Inc., Garden City, New York, 1961.

The Complete Book of Greek Cooking, by Rena Salaman and Jan Cutler, Annes Publishing Ltd., London, 2005.

WEBSITES

http://biology.clc.uc.edu/fankhauser/Cheese/yogurt_making/YOGURT2000.htm: *Yogurt Making Illustrated*, David B. Fankhauser, Ph.D., Professor of Biology and Chemistry,

U.C. Clermont College, Batavia OH 45103. First published December 1980. Revised: 17 December 1993, 5 December 1998, 11 December 1998, 18 April 1999, 20 April 1999, 3 January 2000, 7 September 2000. File "YOGURT2000.htm" was last modified on 24 January 2005.
http://en.wikipedia.org/wiki/Minoan_civilization

MOVIES AND OTHER MEDIA

My Big, Fat Greek Wedding, Nia Vardelos, Gold Circle Films in association with Home Box Office and MPH Entertainment, 2001.

Zorba the Greek, from a novel by Nikos Kazantzakis, screenplay by Michael Cacoyannis, Twentieth Century Fox, 1964.

Family Biography and Photo Album, 2 CDs, Betty Jane Manolakas, circa 2000.